How to live in the Empire of Love

ONLY BELIEVE

by
SUE SIKKING

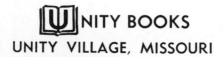

NITY BOOKS
UNITY VILLAGE, MISSOURI

CONTENTS

CHAPTER I

Looking Through

Each of us has a great storehouse of treasures, some of which are just beyond human awareness. We also have the power to bring these treasures into visibility. This power has always been within every person; it came with us from the beginning and no outer condition or situation can take it from us. We cannot do anything to rob ourself of this immeasurable gift. However, we do have the choice to use our God-given powers to the fullest or to let them lie dormant.

Among these treasures is one so profound, so important, that we might say it is our greatest gift. It is the ability to *look through* the visible that is around us to the invisible that is unseen; without this power there would be no progression. We use this faculty all the time to some degree, but we need to use it consciously with love, for the great purpose for which it was created, and for which we were created. It is the pattern of our growth and unfoldment.

In this day in which we live, a day assigned to

us by divine appointment, let us search out our next long step toward making our contribution. Again and again in the history of the human soul the ability to look through appearances has carried the race of mankind forward to new unfoldment and advancement. This ability is one of the greatest forces in human life.

We often call this practice dreaming, yet in our Scriptures it is called vision, and we are told that without it "the people perish." The word *dreamer* is not always a compliment in the world today. Many of us are so convinced of the power of the outer that we think a dreamer is a fool, a misguided thinker. We must remember that our world has always been the outpicturing of the consciousness of man. The mind is the womb of the world, and from this same consciousness we derive the capability to look through appearances to help create and give birth to a new world. Today mankind needs dreamers. Let's look through the confusion, turmoil, and unrest of our time to a new expression of life for every human being, a life based on a new relationship between man and man. Let us be more aware of the secret of looking through, which is second nature to us all.

Moses used the power to look through the endless miles and years of the unknown that spread between Egypt and Jerusalem. Columbus must have looked through the mist and the turbulent waves to unknown continents. Our forefathers in covered wagons must have looked through the forests, deserts, hills, and mountains to an invisible new home. We are forever looking past things as they are to the unseen lying beyond.

We look with our eyes and see the sea and sky and a world of material things, but *look* has another meaning: "to expect." All things great and small have come forth to the outer from this kind of inner seeing. We have come to expect depression, recession, punishment, lack, even dire want. We cannot look two ways at once without confusion and failure. This is why we are warned by the wise of old against double-mindedness, a double heart, or being double-tongued. We are told that a double-minded man is unstable in all his ways and "a house divided against itself cannot stand." To look through is to look beyond any appearance, through the finite to the infinite, through the seen to the unseen.

We look through the rain to the sunshine that lies ahead, through the winter snow and ice to spring that is just beyond, still invisible. We look through the seed to the flower or fruit. We are right now looking through the experiences of life toward the expression of being that is our destiny. We have looked through many difficult times alone and together. We are not the first to meet challenges, assignments, and experiences by looking through them, knowing that life is unfolding and that the hard times too shall pass. We have looked through war to peace, through failure to fulfillment. We look through the infant to the child and make preparations for adulthood. We look through what is at hand in our own life to the invisible life pattern that is beyond, waiting to be reached by awareness.

All the healing that Jesus did was by the power of God, using the ability to look through. He looked through the winebibber, the thief, the harlot to see the real being. He looked always to the unseen, to the ideal being within. True prayer is looking through what seems to be to the truth of life. We look through rain to sunshine, winter to spring, child to adult, because we know they are there. Can we look through things as they seem to be to an invisible expression? Can we *know* that the invisible is always there? This is life—always so much more than we can see with the human eye.

Let our constant prayer be to look through each moment, each experience, to see the good of it. Let us know that humanity has a great destiny "decreed beforehand by a divine will." So let us step forth with courage and faith, going beyond what seems to be to a new world of life, love, and fulfillment. Our scientists tell us that there are processes underway in the universe that are totally at odds with accepted physical laws. "We shall no longer be ruled by cold, narrow rationality. We have a new world."

Let us see through a world of differences, a world of changing times, to a world of love. Love is the greatest power on earth, and world love is easy to understand. It is simply stated in the Golden Rule—to want the good for every human being on the face of the earth as fervently as we want our own. A law of life is that like produces like. The new world will be brought forth by men and women who have the courage to look through appearances to the impossible dream, by those who will know that the dream is *possible*.

CHAPTER II

Don't Be Afraid of Change

This is the age of change. There has always been change; all creation is constantly on the move. We know that life is constantly changing from beginning to end. We know we are not the infants we once were, not the children, perhaps not the youth, but in our innermost part we know we shall be even greater, for it is not yet revealed what we may be. At the moment of birth, all that we are, have ever been, or could ever be came into being. When we were handed to our mother in those first hours of life, in that small body was the child, the youth, the man or woman we are today. We are even now in the process of becoming. Here and now, in the unfolding, growing, evolving movement of Spirit, lies even greater change. Life is always turning, widening, moving onward and upward, even though we may not be fully conscious of the degree to which this is happening. The soul of every human form is in upward flight. At this particular time we are traveling very, very fast. It seems as if we have been loitering along the way, and suddenly we find a discontent, a dissatisfaction, a great inner need. Be not dismayed: it is a divine discontent and a divine dissatisfaction. The Spirit within is moving through all humanity, and it will not let us rest. Civilization is taking a great step forward to cause a new balance that the logical, reasoning mind cannot yet comprehend.

We have all witnessed physical changes and mental development that have carried man forward in every phase of life. Environmental progress has been tremendous, yet what we are experiencing in our innermost being today is strangely different. It is the sign of the Master's hand at work. The change at hand is in the invisible realm of the soul, the freeing of the inner spirit. It is normal growth because it is the natural evolution of all life. The command is to be joyful. The word *joy* comes from an old Hebrew word which means "to be enlarged." If we understand that the changes of the modern world are the fulfillment of the soul and that we are being enlarged, we can go forward joyously!

When we think of change we often think of what seems to be lost or destroyed. *Lost* has its own meaning: the act or fact of failing to gain, or obtain, or use, or utilize. So all seeming loss is our momentary failure to use something that is needful. We may fail to obtain something or gain something from every experience. Everything that happens to us has something in it for us to use. To fail to gain our good does not mean that our good is destroyed; it has always been there and will always be there. It cannot be destroyed; it is always waiting.

We are forever on the move and ever changing. New vistas, new revelations, and new realizations are forever opening in our life, for the vast power of the universe is unfolding all humanity. That which is always within us can never be lost. The realization of our oneness with this moving panorama of life, this universal Power expressing as life and growth, sets our soul free. Our soul is never tied to any condition or situation that we have experienced. Our soul is never tied to any person or persons, no matter how close or dear. No one has "soul rights" to another being. We may assume such a relationship and live within the confines of our assumption for a time, but the soul cannot be detained for long. The soul was born free. No experience can keep us from our onward journey. That which is within us is greater than all that is in the world.

We have oneness with every other soul, knowing that God is within each of us, seeking to release us to our perfect life expression. To love is to set every living soul free to the safety of the unfolding inner Spirit. As we know that oneness and completion can come only from within, we too are set free to fulfill our life pattern and still retain true relationships. We belong to each other, we need each other, but not to possess or trespass. According to the words of Ezekiel

(ASV), the Spirit within said, "I will overturn, overturn, overturn." We will change, change, change until we come into our absolute expression. All changes are to establish us in our own true state of unfoldment.

"Change" comes from the old French word *changler*, which comes from the original Latin word *cambaire*, which means "to exchange." Change always means substitution. We never have a change but something is put in place of what we have had. So change is not only taking something away, it is also giving something new. Change is making room for something else. To make room for all beauty, all newness, we must make an exchange; we must let go of what is to get our greater good. This is the secret of change. We must let go of what we have known so that we may have that which is now ready, prepared for us since the beginning of time. We have made this exchange again and again. We have all put away our blocks, crawled out of our sandbox for a greater expression of life. We have put away our books for the action and doing of life, and now we shall put away the experimenting that we may *be* what we were created to be.

The human being, the highest known creation of God, is continually changing Godward. We must learn to move with the changes, to be at peace while we are making them, and to anticipate the greater good unfolding for us. Change is always progress; don't be afraid of it. If something must be changed, *step out into the change* and see what is already prepared for you. Be willing to change, eager to change, and happily welcome all changes. In truth it will be an adventure to make the exchange. The people who miss life have quit living, loving, and expecting. They have come to a place where they are standing still. They think life is finished and there is nothing to carry them forward, because they will not exchange the old ideas for the new. There are wonderful ways of life, ways we know not of . . . "What no eye has seen, nor ear heard, nor the heart of man conceived, what God has prepared for those who love him."

We cannot stop the flow of life so we must enter into the stream. The world is at a new high. It is calling out for a new way unscaled! We may not be aware of it, but all humanity is getting out of a cage of experiences. We are getting out of a circle of birth to death, failure to failure, war to war, suffering to suffering, and even morning to night. Morning to night isn't the way it is with Spirit. "And there was evening and there was morning." We think of human life as the morning of youth and the evening of old age, but it isn't that way at all. It is always the beginning of a new expression of life. Every moment is an ongoing; there is never an ending. The morning of life always lies before us. It is the evening and the morning of the first day, the second day, the ten-thousandth day, the end of an experience and the beginning of the new moment. We are always on the verge of some-

thing new. Some people are upset if they are
discontent and think they are failing, when in
truth they are only growing. We are never too
old to grow. *Be discontented.* Know that the
ever-unfolding Spirit is opening up a new door
of life.

We are taught about the *now*, and I think we
have missed the point. We can only possess for
the moment. Life is the acceptance of every moment as it comes and goes. All loss results from
holding on to what has passed. We cannot gain
or use the next moment until we have released
the last. We are here to have "life more abun-
dant." Abundance comes from living the moment and letting it go. It doesn't make any difference whether it is a moment of joy or power,
of completion or what we may mistakenly call
failure. The message is the same: *let go!* Let the
moment of triumph go as readily as you would
let go the moment of seeming failure.

Letting go is of the moment. Nothing is ever
lost. Relinquish the moment as quickly as you
possessed it; even though you may experience a
feeling of loss, you may also experience extreme
joy. Everything you have ever known was only
for the moment. "This too shall pass."

We must learn the secret of possession: to
possess now and then let go, that the next moment may come. Sometimes we shut out wonderful experiences because we refuse to let go of
those at hand. Some people prefer to sit in the
ashes of sorrow, of what has passed, rather than

to accept the new good that is always there. They put the limitation of the passing moment on their new experiences. We are told that we must lose our life to find it. Lose the moment, be willing to let it go. "The old has passed away, behold, the new. . . . "

In 1883 a volcano in the Dutch East Indies erupted. Krakatoa's eruption was the greatest explosion the world had ever known. Fourteen square miles were hurled into the sky. Four hours later, three thousand miles away, the explosion was heard distinctly. Dust rose in the sky for twenty miles, and this dust went completely around the earth. Six months later the sky was green over the United States, the sun yellow, and the air filled with the dust from the volcano. In 1884 scientists went to Krakatoa and found no living thing, not a trace of life; all was bleak, desolate. By 1886 there was an amazing change. There were ferns, flowers, grass, butterflies, ants, sugar plums, mangoes; the island was a paradise. The indestructible life of God in nature is also in every one of us. When the realization of this God Presence fills our whole being, we will know we cannot fail. Nothing can destroy that which is within us. Nothing can hold us back. When we realize this we will come into our heritage and know that God *is* all and *in* all. We accept the freedom of the soul now by loving each moment and accepting the next one!

CHAPTER III

Know Yourself

Long ago, far back in antiquity, it was accepted without question that the Spirit that created all things also lived in that creation. Every tree in the forest had Spirit, every smallest plant and creature, even the sun, moon, and planets were imbued with this Spirit that man called God. As man grew in outer power, building empires, taking prisoners, and making slaves, it was no longer considered wise or safe to reveal the great truth that all were created equal, that in all things the great Creator moved. The knowledge of the moving Spirit within every human form was lost.

We are told that Truth crushed to earth will rise again, for Truth is eternal and cannot change. Slowly this noble wisdom was restored by the truly wise of the world. The Truth of the infinite Power that lives within every human form came from all the great teachers of the world.

Long ago over the door of a Grecian temple

the words "Know Thyself" were inscribed. These words are the secret and mystery of our human life. When we find the secret of self, we find all power. As citizens of a new world, we must be aware of our complete being. A human being is not a loner! We never stand alone. Our function is cooperative. Every living soul is part of a team. There is man, the physical being, the body: eyes, voice, hands, and feet; and there is the moving, throbbing invisible Presence of life and vitality within. This is the living Spirit that moves as faith, love, strength, peace, and power through every cell and organ of the physical being. This is our true Self, our personal portion of universal Power, the everywhere-present One!

This invisible Presence within us speaks through the voice and moves through the hands and feet. It is the love in our heart that rushes out to caress and sustain others. This love's purpose is to reach beyond the personal and fill the world with its invisible lifting power. These two, the physical being and the invisible being, are one in Truth. They were created for movement together in perfect harmony in a world of peace and power. What has happened to us?

Man has displaced his true Self. He has forgotten his true pattern, or it goes unheeded. He gets so lost in the outer self that he has spiritual amnesia and temporarily forgets the invisible power that created him. We were all created to be maintained momently by this power. Human beings must believe in a power that takes care of them constantly, even though they cannot explain it in the reasoning mind. This vast power works for the so-called thief, liar, sinner, failure, and any ordinary or extraordinary human being, but *for an unbeliever the power cannot work.* The Bible promises that all things are possible to him who believes. The unbeliever tries to direct his power instead of working with it. All the time, the good that is ours by divine right lies dormant and waiting for an opportunity to move through us. Love is waiting. Wholeness is waiting. Happiness is waiting. The answer to every spoken and unspoken desire is waiting! And all will wait until we *accept* and *believe.* The true power of the universe is every man's inheritance, and it remains concealed within him until he discovers it, uncovers it, and consciously uses it.

Mankind has suffered under the belief of guilt, failure, and inadequacy. We think we believe at this moment in a world of chaos and turmoil caused by misdirected human efforts. The results of these beliefs are violent agitations of guilt in our mind and emotion. These great inner disturbances rob us of health, happiness, and fulfillment in life. These states of mind hold us to the idea that all life is a battle, so the result is inner war. When we are unhappy and miserable, old ideas of sin and punishment rise from the depths of our subconscious mind; guilt crowds into the mind. We always connect sin with all that *seems* not good. Just the word *sin* causes deep inner fear within the individual. As soon as we think of sin we have two fears: the inner fear of our own mistakes, and the outer fear of the world and its pressing material needs.

Let us dispose of sin once and for all. The fourteenth century author of "Theologia Germanica" said, "Sin lieth in the turning away of the creature from his Creator." Sin means separation. There is no sin except our *not knowing* our own power. We must know that the power deep within us is God's Spirit. The Creator is unfolding the law of the universe through us, and this law does not punish. If we do not know the law of the Presence of life within, we separate ourself from our good for a time, but this separation is never permanent.

All power is in us, as it is in all creation. There is no grander power in the world than that which is capable of flowing through human forms at this moment. The whole of power is given to everyone, for the one Power cannot be divided; it is everywhere present. We call it life. It fills the universe. The principle of life moves easily and freely through the human being who simply cooperates consciously by believing. When the outer and the inner self are consciously one, *this is knowing*. In truth there is no experience or situation in life or mind or feeling apart from this universal Power, which is all power and goodness. This inner knowing is always there and can deal with all experiences perfectly. We must become aware of what is really happening to us in this day of change: *we are moving from not knowing to knowing.*

Knowing the meaning of the time in which we live is greater than all outer wisdom. We are living in a period of expansive revelation. We are witnessing the progression and development of the universal plan. The veil between man and the fullness of life is thinning, and man is beholding a new expression of himself. God screens our human mind from premature plans; until the appointed hour arrives our eyes do not see the things that are before our very face. The hour is at hand. We shall see what will prove to be the fulfillment of the new human being on earth, all good.

Every living soul on the planet Earth today is a part of a new stage of growth, the unfoldment of a whole being with dominion and authority in the inner and outer. This power permeates and fills all life. We are witnessing a great psychological moment in our history. The moment has arrived when the mind of man will know what the soul and spirit of man have known forever. It will be revealed to every living soul through daily experiences from the mighty power in the midst of his own being. The purpose of this power within is peace and progress for all, and it promotes our advancement. This new growth is not of wealth and outer power, nation against nation or man against man; it has nothing to do with rivalry, competition, national or personal strife, outer or personal gain. All humanity is coming to know that the material world with all its wonders is not enough. There is still something within man that is not satisfied or fulfilled.

In the midst of the pressures of the unknown, the uneasiness of mind and soul, we feel as did Tagore, the poet of India, who said: "I thought that my voyage had come to its end at the last limit of my power, that the path before me was closed, that provisions were exhausted and the time come to take shelter in silent obscurity. But I find that thy will knows no end in me. And when old words die out on the tongue, new melodies break forth from the heart; and where the old tracks are lost, new country is revealed with its wonders."

There is always the cusp, the overlap, the residue of the old and the flowing in of the new. We again remind ourself that no change is instantaneous. We are awakening to the truth that the confusion, indecision, and sense of failure are only symptoms of letting go of the old and taking hold of the new. The complete unfolding of mankind has been for this end, to fit together and prepare the body and soul for the full operation of the Spirit of life. We cannot return to the expression of life from which we are moving, any more than the adult can return to being a child. We must press forward into a new world of expression. The universe is an orderly and harmonious system, and we belong to the cosmos. We too were created orderly and harmonious, although our human thinking may deny this. There is much more to us than we know! To quote Tagore again: "Oh fool, to try to carry thyself upon thine own shoulders! Oh beggar, to come to beg at thy own door! ... Whom dost thou worship in this lonely dark corner of a temple with doors shut? Open thine eyes and see thy God is not before thee. ... The traveler has to knock at every alien door to come to his own, and one has to wander through all the outer worlds to reach the innermost shrine at the end. My eyes strayed far and wide before I shut them and said, 'Here art thou!' The question and the cry, 'Oh, where?' melt into tears of a thousand streams and deluge the world with the flood of the assurance, 'I AM!' " We awaken now to the power that has been within us always.

All things are possible with a human being. We are all at one with a tremendous power, yet we have not fully used it. We have built mental limitations and we look around them to a world that is really ours. I AM is the name for God, given to Moses for all generations, and I AM is also in us. When we turn our face, mind, heart, and thought toward this tremendous inner power, everything comes into order and harmony. This temple in which we live and move and have our being is at one with the great One. This physical-spiritual being that we call I AM is the most important being.

The most important being for you is you, at one with I AM. This is the "temple not made with hands." This is the temple of life, joy, happiness, fulfillment, and good feeling; it is God's only means of full expression. You are the center of all life for you. All right relationships with others come through you and can come in no other way.

There is a stronger power in our life than business, success, income, where we live, or our relationships; yet all these have their place and are precious. Fulfillment depends on what we think of ourself. The new life pattern will be built on our relationship with self, and expanded through our relationships with all other human beings. All of us are creations of God and we are filled with beauty and wonder. Every step we take is a step toward the freedom of our soul, toward all that we are to accomplish in our new freedom. We are never alone; we are members of a heavenly body, the cosmos, the order and harmony of the universe. We must listen and be guided from within, listen to the still, small voice of God, the intuition, the hunch, what St. Teresa called the "shepherd's pipe." The shepherd takes care of the sheep with his pipe, perhaps a flutelike instrument. The sheep know the sound and are therefore calm; we too should know the sound of our Shepherd and know that nothing can touch us. This voice is not the voice of the human mind with its reason and logic; it is the voice of the heart, the voice of the Spirit within yearning for completion.

Every experience, desire, need, and longing is the pressing forth of this mighty inner power.

Our old good is falling away; it sufficed for the time. Nothing is ever lost, for a higher good comes to take its place. Change always leaves something behind and brings something forth. All of us are ready for the revelation of the invisible One, and we are being prepared to accept it—all religions, all nations, all races. Faith and believing are always backed up by a hundred times more than seems to be. Defeat comes only when we accept things as they seem to be. Remember that *much more* is always ready and waiting for us.

Do not judge by appearances. Nothing is ever as bad as it appears to the human eye. It is never too late. We are never too old, too sick, too poor, or too much of a failure. Let us take all barriers down. Barriers are the thoughts of our outer mind that believes in lack and separation and is forever fearfully seeking ways and means to bring about good, *when good is already here and ours for the believing.* Do not try to find out how the invisible power works—just claim it and it will take care of all needs. Give thanks! The finite mind cannot understand the infinite. Believe in believing. Become as little children. Believe without question in a power that takes care of us. *Accept nothing less!* When there is any challenge to meet in life, declare the living truth: "God is in the midst of this." George Washington read the oath that was written for him when he accepted the office of President, adding his own words at the end: "So help me

God." Those who do not yet know call their life experiences by limiting names: lost, disgraceful, incurable. Don't accept these terms! Incurable, for instance, only means that nothing *outside* the human form will cure us. The cure is always in us, thus, *in-curable*. This power is ours now, not someday when we learn more or are more advanced. It is not ours because we are good, nor is it taken from us when we seemingly make mistakes. It is ours because it belongs to us and has always been with us; our *believing* sets it free to express in all that we are, think, and do. When darkness fills our life we depend on the power within; when daylight comes we depend on the power within. The command of the new age will be to *listen*. Listen . . . we shall have desires, ideas, directions for fulfillment. Listen! All power is in this very place, within our mind and heart, every moment of every day. All power is ours!

"By love may He be gotten and holden; but by thought never." We cannot find our inner power with the intellect. We may find out about it through the mind, but to experience it and use it we must feel it. To live is to love. Love is life in its fullness. Love is the purest activity of spirit. Love is the drawing, unifying power of life. Love is the way of life, the everyday business of good living. Life is getting up, sometimes on the wrong side of the bed and sometimes on the right; life is sometimes being encouraged and sometimes being discouraged. The poet said, "If you shut your door to all errors, truth will be shut out." All power is in the midst of us, doing all things through us, right where we are in every experience. Our human, reasoning mind says this could not be—people destroy, hate, and kill. But Jesus answered this reasoning in one line: "They know not what they do." The very person we may judge or refuse to help is someone on his way up. Evolution is growth and unfoldment toward conscious knowing. Only by loving can we be set free. Love sees through to the unseen. There is a spiritual Presence in man, activated by love, that destroys mental and physical illness. Mental illness is caused by fear and anxiety, which lead to inner emptiness. Physical illness is the result of not knowing our innate wholeness; this ignorance outpictures in the body, yet it is not lasting.

Do not dwell on old age, whatever your age may be. Aging does not mean deterioration of the body. Aging is part of the experience of living, and the more we live, the better we know how to live. We are virile, vital, and whole, regardless of age. Love is ageless. Age records our movement through and experience of the diversity of life, our evolution and growth. The human mind may have accepted the aging process as something undesirable, but the power that we use to live is the power that recreates, renews, and revitalizes us. Let us love our whole being. Let us praise the life power within, which has been with us since before we came forth from the womb. *Praise* means "to prize." To praise is to magnify, and love is the power that draws, harmonizes, magnifies, and holds everything in its right place. "He who wants to do good knocks at the gate; he who loves finds the gate open."

We have all been chosen to be alive today. We are not here by chance, but by divine appointment. Let us not delude ourself with the mistaken idea that we live in a world of shadow and so-called evil. All experiences are the assignments of growth. Nothing is impossible. We have been given the power for *our* time. Now is that time. We are the people. The unfolding world is the path of life. If we can be less concerned about the mundane, our inner Lord will fit all experiences into their proper place in our life. We are seeing and experiencing the "unhappy business that God has given to the sons of men to be busy with." We must know that through our experiences we are growing. We must plumb the depths of self. We must be aware of the expansiveness of our own soul, the depth of our loving feeling. We have been surface creatures, and now we shall awaken to a "new heaven and a new earth" in us and around us.

CHAPTER IV

Wind of Truth

Each one of us has what appears to be two selves: our everyday, outer self with personality; and the one we were created to be, the self we are unfolding, bringing forth into manifestation with moment-by-moment living. Our purpose in life is to evolve and unfold our being to follow a perfect pattern. This is true of every person on earth, although we may not all be aware of this truth at our present point of expression.

There is a divine plan, though many would deny it for themselves and for others. Yet we have all known deep within that we should accomplish the seemingly impossible. We have believed deep within that we should be alive, joyous, and free. At some point man came to the false belief that this would not happen on earth, but that heaven is after the death of the body; some people even doubt this accomplishment. We have believed that we must do great overcoming to manifest this God-created self. We have believed that to do so would be a long and tortuous experiment, yet we are reminded to "Consider the lilies of the field, how they grow; they neither toil nor spin; . . . Therefore do not be anxious."

Life is to be lived here. We are here. Life has always been *now*, and it cannot be consigned to some other place and time. Life is the experience of learning. We have taken the events of life to be final and unchangeable but in truth everything will come to pass. *The secret is to let the experiences of life pass.* Live daily, die daily to all that happens, and move on. The true unfoldment according to the pattern within us is natural, and it is going on at this moment, wherever we are, whatever we think we are. It is as simple and as profound as the physical growth and maturation of a child. We are in the process of growing up spiritually. Growing up is not finished when our physical growth ends.

Our seeming self is the one that we have been taught we must be. We have been instructed in outer behavior, believing that we bring about our good or destroy it by behavior. "Do this, don't do that." "This is good, that is evil." "What will people say if you do that?" This is traditional teaching, oral or written transmission of information and belief; it is something handed down from the past, *not necessarily true.* Most of our instruction has been contradictory. Some things are called good at one time and evil at another. There is One within us who is greater than we think, more than we have ever dreamed we could be. We are this person that we appear to be, but we are *so much more.* This is the mystery of life. Tennyson says: "Speak to Him thou for he hears, and Spirit with Spirit can meet—Closer is He than breathing, and nearer than hands and feet." We are at one with our true Self.

The living Spirit of God is within us, thus we are one with all creative power. This living power of God is our pattern, our true Self. We have thought that all the living of life is in the outer world, that everything comes from outside ourself, that we of ourself are nothing more than fleshy, sinful beings, full of limitations and fear. The truth is that all we are, have ever been, or can ever be is within us now! That which is within us is "greater than he who is in the world." We are constantly unfolding; this is the pattern of growth. Nothing outside of our own acceptance or reaction can touch us.

We cannot live in the past. We must move with life. A child cannot remain a child, or continue to be ruled by the patterns of the child. The eagle is a wise bird. When it builds its nest, it finds thorns and sharp, jagged bits of branch or stone. Then it covers all these with leaves and grass. It lays its eggs, they hatch, and when it is time for the young birds to leave the nest, the mother eagle scratches away the leaves and grass, and the thorns and thistles make the birds abandon the nest.

The law of life is movement. The young eagles

must leave the nest. We have all felt the sharp, jagged rocks of experience, the nudge to move on. Our nest of growth has been our past experiences of life. Nothing is ours consciously except by experience, but all experience must be left behind that we may move into our next expression of life. We have been in our little circle of experiencing the unfoldment of life, but we have also hedged our life around with rules and regulations, customs, habits, and traditions, thus closing out some of the wide, beautiful world that lies in us and before us.

We can be hampered by beliefs and thoughts that were suitable to our parents and grandparents for their time and experience. We cannot expect these same beliefs to fulfill our needs for unfoldment. The sharpness of life will make us uncomfortable; some of us will experience the utter collapse of our way of life. We can see that many of the pat theories and set ways of our world are being torn to shreds. We are ready for the next step of unfoldment.

Our old religious beliefs of good and evil, our government and politics in which we felt strength and freedom, our hopes and dreams of the security of material wealth and power are all blowing in the wind. Like the young eagles, we do not know where we are going. The nest is gone. Some would have us believe that evil has taken over the world, but it is not evil: it is the powerful wind of Truth. "You will know the truth, and the truth will make you free." God is having His way with us whether or not we understand or like it. The wind of Truth has blown open the gates of the new age. All that is not true, all that is outgrown, no longer useful for the time at hand, is tossed about like dead leaves in the wind.

Now is the greatest time on earth for all of us. We are witnessing the fulfillment of the promise of the Scriptures: every man is becoming one with the wisdom of his own being. One step of our unfoldment is finished. Something new and alive is taking its place. We will no longer read how Truth will be done, we will live it. Every soul is required *to be*, instead of talking about being—to be whole, free, happy, alive, and aware—for there is a new world to be shaped by us.

Everything that happens should make us take a good look at ourself. Our concern is not what others are doing or not doing. *We must each find ourself.* The movement of Spirit within humanity is pressing at the door of our awakening consciousness. We have been locked in the cage of our own thought, and now we are being rudely awakened from our false security in the outer world alone. We are awakening to an unseen power, knowing that all is well. The human story is not coming to an end. We have turned a page to find our true Self waiting for us. H.G. Wells said, "Man's mind is at the end of its tether." When we come to the end of our personal mind we come to God. "Beloved, we are

God's children now; it does not yet appear what we shall be."

As we think of the challenges that lie before us, as we are trying to arrange and rearrange the experiences of life, the great inner wisdom of God is perfectly and beautifully creating each one of us. We are often completely unconscious of the mystery of our own inner process. We may think, plan, devise, contrive, fabricate, and invent, yet the mystery and plan of God is perfectly unfolding in the midst of us. If we know what is happening, we will not delay this unfoldment by questioning or doubting. "Do not be anxious." Our world is not yet finished. Our power to know is the plan of God. Our power to think is the starting point toward knowing that God is creating us every moment. We are expressing continuing creation today.

Man was created in the image of God, and His likeness comes forth as we work with the inner, unfolding pattern. Man is created, man is creative, and creation is always now. We weren't created and left. Creation is an ongoing, moment-by-moment activity. Creation is now; it is ever present and always will be. The law of life is constantly acting, fulfilling, and bringing forth the likeness of God in us, right here, today. If we could only remember this, let go and forever forget the idea that in some way we have to *become* something else, that we have to *do* something more in order to become this something. We already are an unfolding expression of the Spirit of God within.

We need to learn to live joyously in order to have full ability to do all the things necessary to our fulfillment. We must let things happen if we are to have happiness. The outpicturing of our inner image follows the pattern of all life. We have the power to bring forth His likeness. We have the power to *image*, and bring forth the likeness of what we image. Our whole world comes forth as a result of the power to image.

Just trust. "No man can serve two masters." "No one can carry two melons in one hand." "It is impossible for man to mount two horses or stretch two bows." We must be free to unfold the living Spirit from within our own being. *Now is our time!* Let us not be distracted by cares about outer things, although they seem to surround us. Take no anxious thought; it hinders the flow of Spirit. *Release.* How do we release fears and doubts? How do we take no thought? By trusting in God. The Power that created us lives in us and is moving through us. We have the ability to change our mind, to repent. We were also given the power of renunciation and acceptance, the power to say yes or no. True righteousness is what is right for us, revealed to us by our own inner feeling and knowing. Release, let go of all fearful thoughts, and see what God can do through you! Doors will open, ways will be made clear. The mind cannot carry forth the new creation if it is filled with unanswered questions.

Choose this day . . . not which way you are going, for this is not revealed to any of us at this time; but choose to become quiet and believe that God is with you, just as you are. We do not get an awareness of God by outer learning but by inner believing. He alone can fulfill our nature. Human life is an intimate relationship between the inner spirit Self and the outer expression, between us and our true Self. Let us not be preoccupied with how we will do what seems to need doing. We are not going to do it; it is going to be done *through us* as quietly and as truly as all growth and unfoldment has taken place deep within us since the beginning of life.

We are coming to know new concepts, new realizations, new unfoldments that are almost too great to comprehend in their entirety. There is an unfolding, forward movement, and there is a dropping away—like unto the butterfly from the cocoon, the bird from the eggshell, man moves from not knowing to full knowing. Nothing can change this unfolding pattern of life. No worry or fear or prayer can hold back this experience. "I am fearfully and wonderfully made." The very experience, condition, or situation that is ours today is an integral part of the way, the dropping away of the old and the coming forth of the new!

Our experiences are like the tempering of steel, the pruning of a plant: they lead to the fulfillment of the soul. They are the preparation for the next moment to be lived. Today is the most glorious day we have ever lived. The almighty Presence is unfolding in us now. *Today defeat is not seen as defeat.* We move with the rhythm of the universe, Spirit unfolding. Our two selves are at one, that we may move in unison with the here and now.

CHAPTER V

The Stone the Builder Rejected

The human race is made up of builders by trade. We have built a magnificent world with almost magical skill, adapting things of the natural world to the uses of daily life. We have built cities, founded governments, created educational institutions, built the world of business and trade. We have built recreation centers, as well as places to work, and religious organizations wherein we might worship. We have built dynasties and empires, following the pattern of a never-ending unfoldment.

We have built our world and affairs with invisible powers, from dreams and visions created and nurtured in the storehouse of our innermost being. We have built the environment in which we live—our family life and all of our affairs— from the invisible essence and substance of mind and heart. Our body also is sustained by this invisible Power. When we were created we brought this invisible building material with us. We have done the building with faith, believing in the dream when we could not see what stretched before us. We have moved forward with great trust. Life is an adventure. We have listened to the inner voice of wisdom for inspiration, often without being consciously aware of its presence and power or what it truly is. We have drawn from the central storehouse of ideas. We have used the gift of imagination, our picture-making power. We have accepted the law of unfoldment and used the Power within us which brings everything to fulfillment. We all know that desires, hopes, and yearnings are the movement of Spirit for expression. We have had the faith to finish our creations, and we must always move on to more glorious ones.

Man has wagered his life many times for his achievements. He has brought forth good with zeal, interest, and enthusiasm. He has been filled with the power to acquire, and he has acquired outer authority, fame, riches, and honor. People from every nation and walk of life, from every race and background, have done all this with the invisible creative Power in us all. *The world is here before us in testimony of man and this invisible Power*. Man's mind is the womb of the world. The evidence sprawls from the smallest gadget to the dynamic space capsule. Yet somehow we are a little tired, like children who have played too long. Today in the midst of a fantastic world something is unfinished, and all humanity is searching to complete it. There must be something more to fill the void of life!

What is lacking? We know it is something of great importance. Our soul knows that the answer is imperative to the fulfillment of life on earth. We know there must be a definite reason and purpose for the pressing need within us, and we must find out what it is.

We are told in Psalms: "The stone which the builders rejected has become the head of the corner. This is the Lord's doing; it is marvelous in our eyes. This is the day which the Lord has made; let us rejoice and be glad in it." We have not rejected the ability to dream, think, and plan, for this vital energy is necessary to the fulfillment of life. This has been the source for the creation of our outer world, built with spiritual building stones: faith, trust, wisdom, imagination, all the faculties of mind and heart. But in our building we have rejected the perfect stone, cast it aside. Why? Was it because we were evil or unworthy? Does this mean we made a mistake, that we failed to build aright? Have we "sinned," and are we being punished? No, a thousand times no! All is in divine order. "This is the Lord's doing; it is marvelous in our eyes." The unfolding law of God is always divine order. Is all the confusion and seeming turmoil in the world a part of an infinite plan? Yes! Regardless of the measure of our reason and logic and the beliefs we have accepted as true, there is human growth as true as the unfolding of the flower and the ripening of the fruit.

Mankind has not been ready for the fullness

of life, any more than a child in kindergarten is ready for college. Man was sent out to grow and unfold, to experience, to fall down and get up. He went forth to learn, to *know* by living, by finding all the answers, drawing from the great storehouse within; by feeling the fullness and the emptiness, experiencing the darkness and the light, since God made both! We were not ready. We are only now developing to the place where we can successfully use our inner Power for good.

We have been in the school of life. We have endured and moved through uncertainties, dangers, hazards of all kind. We have uncovered power beyond power, reached through all security to find the highest adventure, to live, to bring forth, to touch the illimitable, infinite real of full expression. This has been our assignment, to see our dreams and hopes shattered, to feel sadness and failure, to touch the clouds and know success, all good. These have been steps in our unfoldment that we might be prepared for a new age, a world beyond this world called "a new heavens and a new earth" here and now.

To wage wars, to overcome and be overcome by force, have been the experience of each soul. The soul experienced war and tribulation because we must know that these do not satisfy, that there is more beyond this moment, and we must go forward to our true fulfillment. The soul is ready for spiritual maturity, and a new expression of life is prepared for us. We may not be fully aware that this is true but it is God's appointed time within us. We do not sing operatic arias after our first music lesson. For generations we have been under rigid training for this new world. Every creation of God has evolved. We do not make mistakes or fail in Truth, we unfold and outgrow. All the experiences we have had in our spiritual growing-up, all that we have called sins, miseries, troubles, and problems have brought us by diverse paths to this point in time. Every experience we have ever had has brought us to this moment, and each will take its right place in our soul as a part of a divine plan.

Love was the stone the builders rejected. Love is the power that holds everything in its right place, from the tiniest insect to the planets in the sky and universes beyond sight. Love holds the soul and body together. Love is the fulfillment of the law of life. Love is the greatest commandment of all. We are commanded not to be loved but to love. What flows from us returns to us increased and multiplied. The only answer to unfolding life today is our ability to love. To love is to be true to our own wisdom and guidance, to know that we are each "one of a kind," unique. We have our own inner pattern. We are to recognize this perfect truth as we look at every other human being. We must listen to the still, small voice, the inner-teller that comes through us as feelings, desires, and needs. To love is to want freedom for every other human being to follow his own inner voice, as we want to follow our own. To interfere with another person's unfolding inner pattern is trespassing. To let others turn us from our inner guidance is to be trespassed against!

As we have been moving slowly, sometimes unconsciously, into this new realm of being, we have come to honor, and we are even now coming to a greater realization of, every person's heritage and importance. Each day we must become more aware of the one Spirit, the universal energy and essence that gives us all life. "He who is of God hears the words of God."

Love, when we want another's good as we want our own, will fill our heart and mind and extend to every part of our life and world. Love is the feeling of unity, oneness, yet not uniformity. All of us must be free to express our unique life pattern. Love is not concerned with race, nationality, religion, or difference; it is concerned only with life and living, and that we be what we were created to be. In reality we are all one, infused with the one universal energy we call life. Life is our most precious gift, common to all and above all differences. Love is the power that protects and keeps life in its true place.

Love is becoming the cornerstone in all building toward the new world. Love must be the cornerstone in every expression of life. We are moving into a new world of love. Look for it all around you. Don't think of it as just personal, physical love, as precious and beautiful as this is. Love is man's true attitude toward man. We cannot love God without loving each other, for humanity is of God and God is in humanity. To say "I love you" to those we know is the same as saying "I love you" to a stranger. It is saying: "I bear witness to the God-presence within you. I know you are one with me." Love sees only the perfection which glows from within the one who loves. Love is the revelation of wholeness, clearly seen when we look through the eyes of love. If we look with eyes of differences and unconcern, we cannot see the supreme proof of our oneness with each other. Only with the eyes of love can we see oneness, for only in love is there no separation.

Time, space, failure, misunderstanding, life experiences cannot dim the strength and power of love in the new realm of mankind. We shall find that there is no body to heal and no problem to solve; there is something to know. This something has been within us always; it is a power so great that we cannot fully comprehend it by thinking. By *knowing* with feeling, without a doubt, the power wells up within us, free to flow through us and flood us with new life and vitality. All that man has brought forth on earth cannot restore his own being, but love can. The cornerstone of love was put into place when we were created. Love is universal power in action. Love will stream through every cell of the physical body, hence there can be no lack of life. Don't be afraid to love. It will be the *only* way.

We can find any answer with love. Every day is full of loveliness, but we can only know it with love. Let's begin by feeling the love inside ourself and everywhere around us. To love is to send forth, in every thought and word, the belief in goodness, the belief that all is well in spite of appearances. We need to love each other, for *we need each other.* The man in the air is helpless without the man on the ground. The man in the city starves without the man in the country. All daily human needs—lights, heat, water—depend on someone somewhere. Let us love and honor our unknown benefactors.

Send love to people everywhere. Send it to those who hate and destroy, to those who are seemingly lost in a purely material world. Send it to those in public offices and private businesses. Send it, not to faces or to names, but to souls everywhere. The important thing is to see what will happen to you, even though you cannot fully measure what your love can do for humanity.

As the stone that is to be the corner is put into place, all differences fade away. We honor the heritage of another's race, nationality, and religion as much as we honor our own. In love there is no Jew, Christian, Buddhist, or any other sect or difference. We are all one race, the transparent race of God, that fills every person with its invisible Presence.

Every country has been a setting in which a great play of mankind has taken place. Each country has given its beauty to the fulfillment of the whole; slowly yet truly we have become one world. So many of us think that as the new world comes we must let go of the near and dear of the past, but the Scripture says that everyone who finds this kingdom within is like a householder "who brings out of his treasure what is new and what is old." Every part of life has been part of the preparation for the new building of love and truth. We shall use all of our experiences, old and new, in the new life.

Time, space, failure, misunderstanding cannot dim the strength and power of love. Whatever you think about the world today or the inhabitants of it, send forth your love to all, everywhere. Love is an attachment, a connection with every other being. *Love is God's restoring power in the body of humanity.*

Love attaches you to everyone, but in reality you are loving the same One in all. No longer can love be focalized. Learn that love is a lifeline, and tie many lifelines to yourself. Love cannot be contained. True love sees the beloved everywhere. A research foundation studied love; here are some of the findings: "A power that doesn't cost a cent to produce . . . most powerful weapon against disease . . . more easy to stockpile than steel . . . makes you live longer and be happier—*perhaps man's only hope of survival.*"

Love is the fulfilling of the law of God. Now love shall become the cornerstone of every life, and God's plan will be fulfilled. Let us not forget that love is the greatest expression of invisible Power on earth today, and let us also remember that it was understood by those who recognized its importance long ago. They wrote: "And I will show you a still more excellent way. If I speak in the tongues of men and of angels, but have not love, I am a noisy gong or a clanging cymbal. And if I have prophetic powers, and understand all mysteries and all knowledge, and if I have all faith, so as to re- move mountains, but have not love, I am noth- ing. If I give away all I have, and if I deliver my body to be burned, but have not love, I gain nothing. . . . Faith, hope, love abide, these three; but the greatest of these is love. Make love your aim."

The fullness of love can come only to the soul that has experienced the living of life, with its contrasts and assignments. All that has come to us in every moment of living is part of the growth of the soul toward completion and ful- fillment. From the deepest experiences comes the state of being that receives the greatest ful- fillment and attainment. Remember the words of the poet about a lily on the breast of the river: "Oh marvel of beauty and grace, did you fall right down from heaven, Out of the highest place?" And the reply of the lily: "Nay, I came not down from heaven; none gave me my saintly white. It slowly grew in the darkness, out of the deepest night. From the ooze and the slime of the river I won my beauty and grace. Great souls fall not, my poet—they rise to the highest place."

Every day of living has brought us to this, our day. Each moment was a moment of growth toward God's destiny for us. Don't judge your past, or the past of another, just love and believe! True believing moves into *knowing*, and knowing is the secret of all life.

CHAPTER VI

The Empire of Love

Life is not a question mark; life is an exclamation point of wonder when we know without doubt that we are limitless, fearfully and wonderfully made! All the power there is, all the presence there is, all the conscious awareness we have ever had or could ever have is one life, and God is that life. God is love. This is illumination! We are stopping our talk *about* God and letting Him be truly alive in us. We are becoming aware of the great pulse of God beating within us. We call it love, but in all our experiences of human love we have never touched such a breathless, exquisite feeling and knowing. We anticipate this feeling even before it is truly ours because it is pressing upon us from every side.

True illumination is not just mental or intellectual. It is an awakening to a deep inner *Source* from which the mind and intellect draw their power. True illumination is an inner awareness, a flow of universal energy, a knowing. It comes when all sense of limitation is swept away and a sense of well-being prevails. This sense of well-being is not based on either the wealth or knowledge of the outer world, but on an invisible inner essence.

This illumination that fills our being causes outer evidence that seems new but in truth is as old as time. It is a further release of the one and only Power; it is divine order. All humanity is being moved with newness of life. The release of this powerful energy through our soul will change not only our body, the state of our affairs, governments, economics, methods of education, and relationships with others, it will also change the attitude and conception of the whole world. We are told clearly that this change will affect "a great multitude which no man could number, from every nation, from all tribes and peoples." In other words, our whole existence will change, because we will all be "new creatures."

The soul of mankind longs for freedom from the bondage of mind and intellect and the limitations imposed by man's one and only sin: his belief in separation. The new life movement is oneness, unity, union. "One God, one Father, of whom are all things." Even though that knowledge is not in every man, we all are waiting breathlessly for it. All living beings are ready for a new empire, and this empire is being formed even though we are often unaware of its presence and its true implications. An empire is made up of many groups, nations, races, under a single sovereign power. This new world consciousness will have nothing to do with outer, material power or with human logic, reasoning, or fear. When this new empire comes forth we shall understand the words of Jesus, "My kingship is not of this world." The power that will reshape and transform the outer world will come forth from the innermost part of each of us.

This new expression of life has been foreseen and foretold for thousands of years. From the "new heaven and the new earth" of Revelation to the words of Napoleon Bonaparte, uttered in his last lonely reveries on St. Helena, which express the strongest thing in universal history: man's at-one-ment with God. Napoleon expressed his faith in a new world for all mankind when he said: "Alexander, Caesar, Charlemagne, and I have founded empires; but upon what do these creations of our genius depend? They were founded on force and have perished. Jesus alone founded His empire upon love: and it shall last forever."

The empire of love is closer than we know, although to the logical mind it might appear to be just a pipe dream. The strange part is that our outer human expression is never fully aware of the development of the soul in the secret place within. Every one of us will "die" to the limited personal self we think we are and become alive to a completely new being, a superman or superwoman. This is a tantalizing glimpse of what is now at hand.

The empire will have an emperor. An emperor is one who is in command, in order, a supreme sovereign, supreme being. Our emperor will not be a man or a woman, but the one Power that dwells in every man and woman. To worldly wisdom such a thought may be a shock. "How could that be?" Because we have chosen men to rule us and they have failed again and again, and yet again! Every soul must recognize the inner presence of God, familiarly called "Something." We know there is an inner voice that tells us and moves us. We are speaking of it when we say, "I knew I should," or "I had a feeling about it," or, "Something told me." "Your ears shall hear a word behind you, saying, 'This is the way, walk in it.' " Our outer mind has been known to drown out this still, small voice because of its need for evidence of appearances. As we move into the empire of love we shall all listen to and hear the inner wisdom.

Eventually we shall recognize a greater invisible empire over all monarchies, democracies, and man-made rulerships of every kind. We will not be ruled by fear, separation, or the limitations of logic and reasoning, which always end in nothingness unless balanced by the one great Cause. There is a greater expression of life than we have accepted. It is here and now. We are just beginning to *live*. Our five senses and their wisdom have not touched the largeness of the universe. The limited wisdom of the world is foolishness with God. We may have believed with our conscious mind that we have touched all knowing, but in the past we have barely scratched the surface of knowing. To accept the appearances of our outer world as totality or reality is to dwell in illusions. A new and higher form of consciousness is truly manifesting in the human race. From this new consciousness will come the new world. We are "being born again" into a new and exciting experience of life. The fullest awareness is emerging, and it is a life pattern for all.

God within expresses as love. Love is God, for God is love! Love is God in action. Our new expression of love and life will be so great that it will justify the waiting, the experiences, the long-seeming agony of birth. The coming forth into complete conscious awareness of our new faculty of pure knowing is always sudden and instantaneous. Our full mental realization of Truth is not instantaneous; still, the full awareness and conviction can come in a moment, "in the twinkling of an eye." We begin to know some strange new feelings without outward causes. Little by little, we have a sense of release from what had overwhelmed us. Limitations are swept away, sometimes one by one, but they all go. We do not quite comprehend the release and lightness of pure Being, but we find that we are now fearless. Soon we become conscious that this life, this moment we are now living, is both free and eternal.

All that we have called "sin" will be no more,

for sin is separation, and there cannot be separation in Oneness. All that we have known of the human, the outer, is illumined in a new light. Our new human being will not be like the old one, any more than a man is like a newborn baby. The new race will possess the earth. Millions of voices in many languages have earnestly prayed for two thousand years, "Thy kingdom come, Thy will be done, on earth as it is in heaven." *Let us awaken and know that our prayer is now answered*! The kingdom of love and peace is here within us, and we are in the process of setting our mind and heart free to explore it.

The law of love that governs all life cannot be broken. Love is the irresistible force in the universe drawing everything into its perfect expression. We are told by the wise ones that the infinite invisible substance congregates and makes the next highest expression of life. This congregation in divine order is love. In God's divine plan of development, the tiniest particles gather together, the protons and electrons congregate, drawn by the irresistible force of love, to form an atom. The atoms congregate, drawn by the same irresistible force, to form molecules. The molecules are drawn together to form cells. These cells congregate to build a body. Love is the irresistible force that is natural and harmonious and holds all in perfect form. It is the magnetizing, harmonizing, unifying power on every plane of consciousness. Love unites and causes the next higher expression in every instance. Mankind, unaware of the fullness of love, has believed in division and separation, and therefore did not congregate. *God's law does not allow us to know the greater power of love until we are ready for its fullness.* Every soul will respond to the mighty force of love. We will be drawn together. We will follow the perfect pattern of humanity. We will let divine order, the fullness of God, be established in us "on earth as it is in heaven." The new race, the next higher expression of life, is pressing upon us. We have been prepared by deep experiences for this time, and we will not fail.

Oneness of every human being with every other human being is the process growing in our mind and heart and world. To some people, the thought of being one with all mankind is repulsive, since they do not outwardly know every other human being. They need to know that we are all different forms of the same substance, and that the good of all depends on the fulfillment of the law of Oneness. We have not believed it possible to be united because we have experienced separation and difference. But there is always an ending and a beginning of every new phase of life. Now we must know our oneness. We cannot stop growth, which is to unfold the God-human.

Let us heal all separation and division. We have found ourself at the beginning of an age, experiencing separation and division. The institutions of the world fall apart, the minds and hearts of the people remain unfulfilled, as long as any degree of separation prevails from the inner realm of Spirit, in the knowledge of our invisible Oneness. We have experienced the cells of our body falling apart, sickness and disease running rampant, and these cause us to return to wholeness and completion as the divine law of life. We must recognize that we need each other! Love is the only power. Love is God's act of life, from the smallest atom to the completion of a race. Oneness is not uniformity, it is unity of soul, mind, and body.

We do not congregate by uniformity, or by being bound to one another. Congregation does not require that we be identical, like peas in a pod. We congregate *in an inner feeling and knowing that at all times, under all circumstances, we are aware of our relationship with every other human being.* Congregation has nothing to do with loss of free choice. It is the doorway to true freedom. It is an invisible completion that makes us all one in an inner, invisible way. All mankind is safe, for the awareness that there is only One is complete within us all. Truth is the same in every religion. There is one power in every human form, called by many names. In Buddhism it is called *Tat-Tvam-Asi*, which means "I am he, Thou are that." In Hinduism it is called *OM*. In Judaism, the words given to Moses were "*I am that I am.*" To Jesus it was "*the Father.*" To Paul it was "*Christ in the midst of you*," and to John it was *love*.

The outer things of the world come and go—babyhood, childhood, maturity. There is not-knowing, learning to know, and knowing. We have experiences, growth and changes, yet our inner unfoldment is changeless. What we call change is a moving forward of the one and only Power in our heart and affairs. The pattern of the seed never changes, but the pattern unfolds toward complete fulfillment. *Change is new unfoldment of the essence that never changes.*

Let us not cry loss or believe in loss. Nothing is lost, only changed in form. The irresistible force of love gathers, holds, congregates. It is the congregating that causes the higher and higher unfoldment. Love is a universal gathering-together.

Could love rule the world? Could the structure of society be maintained if the spirit of love and compassion were general? Could we have a world without need of outer law, order, and force? The consciousness of mankind in the outer is dual, what the Bible calls "double-mindedness." Yet undreamed of is a society, an empire of love in the process of being unfolded, where human beings of all races and tongues can live in peace and progress and be free to express the full image from within. Modern man and woman may not at this point believe in a world ruled by love if they continue to judge from the outer, but they will experience it. It is closer than we know. We have considered the small expression of love as we use it, individually and collectively, to be *all love*. We are now aware that love is the cosmic power that holds everything together, the harmonizing, unifying power of the universe. Some may say: "What is the use of thinking such a thing? It is physically and mentally impossible to draw all mankind into one circle of love." But dreamers are those in whom love has achieved its supreme triumph. The dreamers are those who will know true freedom, and those who will love when there is nothing visible to love; every member of humanity will become a dreamer of love.

Everything that has come forth in the manifest world had to be thought about and believed by those who dreamed. Let us begin to think about such a society, such a time, such a race, such an empire, and it will surely be manifest, for it already *is*!

Could there be a time of unity and oneness all over this planet, with international postage, international coinage, international language? Could this language be "love," the importance of every human being as something special, above and beyond differences of heritage and custom? *We* must first accept it in *our* heart and mind, plant it in our consciousness and in the consciousness of all mankind. We must first establish it in faith, for this has been the divine law of God since the beginning of time. Those who live in the empire of love will know that in the beginning *we were all one*. The divine law of

God is changeless. "God has ways we know not of, His wonders to perform," wrote the poet Cowper. Let the empire of love begin with us right now, "for the love of Christ controls us."

CHAPTER VII

Builders of the Empire

The builders of the new empire are all over the world, in every nook and corner. Since this empire will *first* be an invisible oneness in the mind and heart of every person, we are unknowingly in the process of building the empire right now.

The builders are carriers of love. Those who carry love bring peace, for love is peaceful. The whole world will soon recognize the leadership of love. All of us will know that our Creator *is* love, and that this quality dwells in the human form. We are unconscious of the activity of life if we don't know and understand this.

The empire will be like no empire of the past; this is a way unscaled, a state of being never before attained by man. The mystery of the new kingdom on earth will be based on every man's conscious awareness of himself. "Know thyself" will be the password for our time. Each of us is a developing, unfolding expression of the great Creator. Unfoldment is not a finishable process nor is it a goal; it is a journeying that is never complete until oneness is established, "on earth as it is in heaven." We cannot even imagine the good that lies ahead. It is sealed from our human knowing and only revealed moment by moment, as we live each day.

Know yourself, and know your relationship with every other member of the human family. Know that the other person—whether he be friend, enemy, loved one, or stranger—is a part of you. Every other creation is an expression of the one life; to know this is to become aware of the secret of all life. This is the Truth that "will make you free"—free from the bondage of not knowing, no longer ignorant of life and relationships with each other. The soul of us knows there is a place, a condition, that is perfectly satisfying and yet progressive, real, and fulfilling for the dwellers therein. The purpose of man's sojourn on earth is to find this place. It is the need that springs eternal in the human breast, the holy quest. This urge has carried man to the four corners of the earth and to the moon. Still unsatisfied, man has turned to inner space. We are finally on our way, and a clearer outline of the new empire is growing in our mind and heart.

Everything that is happening to us individually or to mankind in general is to put us on a unique path, the true path of life that Jesus called "the Way." Everything is bringing us to the realization that we were created for something much greater than outer success or failure, wealth or poverty, health or sickness, war or peace. We were created for completion.

We are meant to move forward to unfold our God-self, the living being we are in embryo straining to grow and be born. We do not find the full secret of life immediately because we must unfold in divine order, moment by moment, to come to completion. We hold fast to tradition, the beliefs of the past, and these beliefs are the icy hands that hold us back; they are obsolete in the new world. It is hard to grow up at any level of consciousness. We move a short way and we attain something, and we say, "This is it!" But the unfoldment and fullness of life continue into infinity, beyond all we can think or imagine. We have stopped short; we have said: "I am here. I have arrived." No soul, no nation can stop here. We cannot stop because the unknown, the "so much more," lies ahead. We are on the move. Never mistake a resting place for the ultimate goal.

The greatest detriment is for us to stand still, to give up, or to think we have arrived. We get too rich, too happy, too wise; or we get too frustrated, too poor, we have too many challenges, and we give up. Whatever causes us to stop, no matter how seemingly legitimate the reason, is destructive, for stagnation sets in. Stagnation means "foul for want of motion," not active. We must pick ourself up, gather ourself together, and move forward.

There is an orderly cosmic rhythm. When we move with this rhythm, we move toward our own completion. This generation is in the process of making the greatest step forward mankind has ever made. *We are the builders of the new empire.* We are in the process of freeing our inner power of love. God is love, so we are building God's empire.

Millions of people are finding their God-self deep within. They are moving from center to circumference. They are holding fast in faith when they cannot see God's good everywhere. They move in every crowd. They may be unrecognized by those who seek in the outer alone, but their numbers are growing by leaps and bounds. They are not fully aware of their own assignment. They sit in every group of people today. They pass us on the street. They are being drawn together, for like attracts like. They are holding fast to the realization of a power within that takes care of all that concerns everyone. They hold fast to peace, their souls are filled with joy. They may waver and tremble, but they tremble because something tremendous is taking place. As they tremble, their world sounds a deep note of harmony and courage.

Today many brave and true people are walking through tribulation, the "pressing" that is a part of our time. Again and again they have pressed through each experience that has assailed them. They pass each place of doubt again and again. They move each day with greater strength and poise, because they feel love and sureness, they hear the inner rhythm to which they are keeping step. They move momently. They do not always know how, they do not always see their way, *but somehow they know*. They will see the way open before them. Completion is within them, and they *know* it will be. The doubts come that they may continue to walk and grow strong, until they walk into the kingdom of God within their own being.

Words of destruction, failures, threats that God will punish, or the fact that the outer world seems to be Godless, do not influence the builders, because *they know*. They may not have proven it fully, but their souls know. They have found love, although they may call it peace, contentment, the right place, or answered prayer. Most people refer to the power within as a feeling, "something," simply because they cannot fully understand or explain the invisible with words. The feeling and knowing of oneness may be beyond the scope of words.

We who have found an inner peace live freely, without fanfare or undue attention. We touch the shores of peace and joy when we are aware of an inner Presence. We who find this inner love are so enriched with more love that we understand the true meaning of joy. We may not be considered by the world to be wise or great if we find love as an inner power, but we will be loving. We may have little or no understanding of philosophies, we may remain undisturbed by conflicting theologies, but the power within is the unsurpassed power. "Love one another" is the slogan of the new empire, and we shall know what cosmic love can be. This does not mean that we become like others, it means that we honor them and know that each one plays a part in the divine plan.

Napoleon reminded us that empires built on force do perish. Empires built for a favored few perish. The intellectualism of Greece existed for the favored few, and beneath the glittering edifice of arts and letters lay the dungeons of the slaves. It was the same in Rome. We may believe that our modern civilization's false god is outer power and wealth, but in truth all good belongs to man, even that of the outer world. Outer expression has only to be balanced in love. There are yawning gulfs between person and person that only love can bridge. We have worshiped empty gods in the outer, but this was necessary so that we might know the only true God, never to be misled again. We are always in the presence of our true God; His power in us is breath and life. We have always been one with this power; the difference is that now we are beginning to know it. We are beginning to realize that we have never brought forth anything without the power of God, which is love.

Love is the substance that holds everything together. It is in love that we recognize our unity and oneness. It is imperative that we all know true love. The assignments and difficulties of our time will continue until we know our relationship with all life. This new flowing life comes through us when we let go and are love-possessed.

It would be impossible to like or to understand every other person in the world. We cannot hope to like them all, or to be like them. The real separation of the old consciousness and the new is not whether we like or dislike, but do we know who we are? We often do not recognize others as a part of ourself. It does not solve anything to destroy our enemies. "A man's enemies are the men of his own house." Our enemies are only in our mind, and love transforms them to be our friends. We are not alike in the outer but we are created one in the inner. There is but one Spirit, one Power, one breath, and one life. To be one with each other in Spirit and in purpose is to be held together for the fulfillment of life on earth, unity without uniformity.

The great gulf between men and love is closing. We know we are all one, yet each of us is whole in himself. It is impossible to be alike. Every soul has a contribution to make to the new empire, and it must be made individually. We who would build the new empire will know each other, we will be acquainted with all other dwellers on this planet. Our good must be held together with love, which is oneness in action.

When we love, we want the good of all mankind as well as our own good. We do not sacrifice our good to be at one with others, nor do we want others to sacrifice their good to be at one with us. The good of all humanity is held together by the one Presence of love. We must love our own God-being and our own pattern. We shall never be free until we set every person free, physically, mentally, and spiritually. When we are true to ourself, we free all others to fulfill their own God-pattern. It is as simple as a seed: no matter how many varieties of seeds there are, each seed is true to its own pattern, its own God-creation.

The only thing that separates us in the outer is the nature of our education, our background, the beliefs we learned in our particular environment; this is "just the width of a thought." These are all circumscribed by the particular time and place into which we were born and lived. We are now moving into a greater expression of life beyond the confines of our own little backyard, beyond the limitations of our past beliefs and teachings.

How do we start as builders of the new empire? We must begin with ourself. Don't say, "If I love people they will take advantage of me, they will take away my good." If you truly love, no one can touch your good. In love *you* are the "captain of your soul" and the master of all that happens to you, the keeper of all that has been given to you. How can we know what will happen in an empire of love when we have never even tried more than the smallest part of love and understanding? This is the adventure of the new race, not necessarily to know, but to move forward without effort or question.

Since the beginning of recorded history our world has been based on the unfolding of mankind. There was a pattern of life based on "an eye for an eye, a tooth for a tooth." It has been a pattern of growth, development, failure, setback, and seeming cross purposes. We have based part of our life on war, hatred, invasion, division, and conquering; with every experience of this kind we have left a little part of the old self behind, as we grew into a new being. These experiences have brought all of us to a place of development where at last we are ready for love and oneness with the whole world. It is significant that no matter where we go, every path leads unerringly straight to the God-self within. No matter how diverse the experiences of life may seem to be, the destiny of life will be completed. In the new world of love there will be no war, no need to fight for peace, for man without question will share his common good.

Let us bring alive the words of Umberto Giordano: "The consciousness of all hearts is to restore all people, to gather up all the tears of the victors and the vanquished and make a world pantheon where all men attain their noble ideals and are united with all mankind . . . where all men would gather in silence and, with one kiss, embrace all men with love."

Let us love one another . . . turn the other cheek . . . resist not evil. If history has anything to teach, it is that nothing has ever been healed or solved by harshness or condemnation. Right now there are ministers teaching love and oneness to murderers and other long-term prisoners. They are helping others to find themselves. These persons should come forth from diverse prisons healed and whole, with reformation of heart, mind, and life. Little by little in nations around the world, all will come to understand that unity is our true good and the good of all that we desire and hope for. We have glimpses of the new world empire of love that is being formed in the minds and hearts of men and women everywhere.

How will we build it? We are not going to build the new empire, for it is already within us. We are building our awareness of it. It is waiting to be set free by our knowing and loving. *Love will do the building! Love is justice. Love is understanding. Love is God!* If there is understanding and communication, there will be wisdom and faith, for these are love, and love is the greatest of all. The time is at hand to prove love, for this is God's loving time on earth. We are all one, even if we have not always been aware of it. Someone has worked for every comfort and necessity in our life. There is a hand that pulls the switch for the streetlights in our city. Food has been grown and brought across oceans by strangers. There are people in forest and foundry who shape our desires and outer destinies. Love will make this oneness whole and complete in consciousness.

We have thought that our world has gone mad for money, but this is only temporary, only an experience to awaken us to the reality of our perfect expression: love. All the unseen hands and unknown faces that have prepared our good will be loved. It was not until during the great "blackout" in New York City that I understood fully how most of our good depends on other persons, the unseen providers who are an integral part of our life. Let us love all mankind, seen or unseen. We are knit together and could not live without each other. Let us begin to understand what oneness is, who we are, and who "they" are. Let us know that love binds all people together in the same way that it holds the individual soul and body together, as well as keeping the sun, moon, stars, and planets in their places.

Slowly but surely in our outer world of economics and commerce man has woven a web, unknowingly, that will fulfill God's plan. We will come to a place in the outer where we will find we cannot do without each other. We have cried out about our independence, we have built walls, made laws, closed borders, levied taxes, and made restrictions, but the time is coming when we cannot do without a single being on earth. *No one will be expendable*.

We have made attempts at unity—the United

Nations, the Common Market, the Olympic Games. We may make other attempts and they may fail, but soon we will succeed. Sooner than we dream, in spite of ourself and the working of the outer mind, the perfect plan of God will come forth "on earth as it is in heaven." *God, the One who became many, is becoming One again.* The plans of man will succumb to his destiny, which is the divine plan of our Creator, God. We shall let the fullness of love, the great *congregating* power of God, fill our earth.

Let us prove this for ourself right where we are. We do not have to take on the whole world, but we give thanks for all that we have in our outer world. We send love and gratitude to the unknown persons who are responsible for the shaping of things that we have taken for granted. We simply let love flow through us now toward all the inhabitants of the earth, not just those who are close and dear, but also the faraway and the unknown. Love is caring, wanting the common good of all. Let love fill this moment. Let it flow from you in conscious thinking and true feeling. Know that the reality of life is love, and that the fullness of the new empire of love is ours.

CHAPTER VIII

This Thing Called Love

Love is the theme song of the universe and the power of the new life. People keep talking about failure, regrets, and guilt because the world looks topsy-turvy and seems to be falling apart. We do not understand what is actually happening. Let us quit dwelling on these things, for they have nothing to do with what is taking place. The age of *not knowing* is passing. The outgrown understanding of ourself and God is obsolete and we are ready for new enlightenment and development.

Do not say that world conditions are caused by mankind's failure. If we say this, we speak without knowledge. Don't blame the conditions of your private world on members of your family or people where you work or live. Don't blame conditions on anyone anywhere! They are the result of the tremendous change that is taking place and the new expression of life that is taking us over. The time of unawareness of our true power is coming to an end. We are becoming aware of the physical matter we call "I" and "me" and of our true relationship to all universal power. This change and its results in our life are the purpose for our being alive today. We are not the same persons of yesterday or last week or last year. We are all changing. We may not see the change; we may even seem to be at a complete standstill in many departments of our life. We cannot see the changes on the new path because we do not realize that they are invisible changes from the inward out, part of our true pattern of life. The old pattern may not be completely gone, for there is an overlap called "adolescence." We are in spiritual adolescence. This is a temporary state, for the law of growth cannot be thwarted. We are moving forward on a completely new level of expression.

The law of our life is demonstrated in our relationship with other human beings. The divine design of life is the congregating, drawing, irresistible force of love. Love is the master key. Is it possible to love all humanity? Yes. And it is not blind love, but the love of one whose eyes are wide open. We are wise when we know we are all one. When we seek this wisdom and understanding, love will fill us. There is an old fable that in the beginning man and woman were one being, and they were later split apart. The story of Adam's rib may be a part of this old belief. The first lesson in oneness must be learned by men and women, for each of us is God's masterpiece. The division of humanity

73

into male and female parts is the divine plan of life. Its purpose and principle is to teach complete self-giving and surrender, training for total oneness. Oneness is the utter abandonment of self to God. Man and woman together in love may experience true communion, an awareness of the deepest spiritual realities.

We are so created that it is necessary for man and woman to experience an expression of love beyond the physical. We were created to express cosmic love, which is law, order, and harmony in the universe, including love for the earth and all creations thereon. True love is always harmonic and orderly on every level of expression.

We were created to experience love in its fullness. Human oneness is love; oneness with all power within is love. Human oneness is a foretaste of our true Self, which is at one with every living expression of life. There seem to be insoluble problems and complexities in life, yet love and God and Truth are simple. Love is everyday living. Love is following one's heart; the heart is the direction of God and life. God expects us to love our own indwelling God-self more than we love father, mother, wife, husband, or child. He expects the same from our father, mother, wife, husband, or child. If we are to feel this loving power within us, the most wonderful experience the world has ever known, we must also use our power of detachment from others. To feel and know cosmic love in its fullness ultimately includes all others. Detachment from others does not mean that we lose them, or separate ourself from them. It truly means that we become closer to them. To free one you love is to draw him close. Freedom demonstrates the trust of our oneness.

This beautiful love that enfolds us and fills us should flow from us naturally and easily—spontaneous, full, warm, and feeling in every moment of life, to every expression of life. It flows out to nature—animals, birds, all creatures great and small. *It is unnatural not to love.* When we withhold our love we suffer and destroy ourself. When we fail to share our love, we rob ourself and others of life. If we stop the flow of love, we stop the flow of life. *Love is the reason for life. We have life that we may express love.*

We may at times, in thinking of personal love, decide to quit loving or try to do so, but if we truly love, we cannot quit. We cause our own difficulties by trying to stop the flow of love. Love flows naturally through every creation of God, but specifically through one who is consciously loving. Love is absolutely necessary to life. Some people think that love comes only once, and they give up all love when their "only" love is lost by departure or separation. Since love is necessary to life, they beat upon the door of life with longing, yet obstructing the free flow of love through them again. There is always love. To stifle it is to deny a natural law of God.

Our love is not just for one person or a few

persons. It is for all expressions of life. It is for every phase of living. We love to live, love to work, love to serve; we love our friends. Jesus reminded us to love the stranger and the enemy as well. Love is sharing, eating together, playing together, laughing and crying together. We love being tired from honest work, we love rest and relaxation. Love is all power in action. Love is the power that works for those who love. Love does not work for the one who only seems to love that he may receive in the outer.

The great mistake that we make is thinking that love must be returned. It is *love* that is the power, not those who accept and share love. People withdraw their attention from love too soon, they grow bitter, because they do not understand that love is the drawing power that brings them all good. They think that the love of others brings them their good. Anyone who withdraws love from anyone for any reason remains loveless and leads an empty life of quiet desperation.

People try to love, and that is foolish, because love does not come by trying. Love is free-flowing and impossible to stop without harm. When we manipulate love, we are in for great heartache. If you are leading a life of frustration because you have been hurt or neglected and have tried to let go of love, stop trying to manipulate love. Be interested in your own life and in others. Get to know new people and try to understand them. Take down all the fences built by tradition. There are not some people you should love and others you ought not to love. Such notions were held by people long dead, and they do not belong to the new world, the empire of love. Love all who cross your path, from anywhere on the face of the earth. You may not like them or understand their ways, but love is caring and desiring the highest good for all. The law of God is to love; to like is the choice of the outer.

As you look at all persons as a part of yourself, when you know that your good and their good is bound by immutable laws, you will set free the imprisoned love within you, and you will experience universal, cosmic love. Assume, no matter what your past has been, that you are beloved because you are one with love. "Who seeks for heaven alone to save his soul may keep the path but will not reach the goal. While he who walks in love may wander far, yet God will bring him where the blessed are." In the brave new world love will be the fullness of our good. Why hasn't love been the key to life in the past? We were not advanced enough in the school of experience to trust our greatest gift, *love*.

We have expanded our outer knowledge of the materialistic world. We have been involved in competition and expansion of the outer without being fully aware that we were becoming a new race in a new land of mind and heart. We have not realized that great inner changes were taking place, and we have thus let love and the new age wait outside. We have not yet considered love as a power, much less been aware that it is the most dynamic energy in the universe. We have not known it was the one Power in action.

We were not fully prepared to accept and recognize love as a perfect expression of life and the universe. Love has been considered a troublesome emotion that must be subordinated in the mental and material pattern of life. There are those who believed love made them weak. They did not understand or know that *God is love*. The boy does not know the fullness of life until he becomes a man and experiences it. There must be certain experiences before there is advancement. *Love will open every door!* Poets and dreamers have been the real bearers of oneness, because they are carriers of love. The time has come when all shall know God as love.

There is newness of life in every moment of love, from the holiest expression to the simple love that one has to have in order to cook, to clean, or to garden. There is only one mighty power for this troubled world: it is love. *We haven't even tried love, much less trusted it.* Our time to try love is only now taking shape. Love is trust, and man has needed to grow to the fullness of trust. He has needed more experience, more assignments. Love is faith, and faith is believing when we cannot see, and the man of the past age channeled most of his faith into the material world for wealth and power. These were his lessons to learn: Love is security, though security has been deeply rooted in the material world.

Love is understanding. It is the invisible and powerful essence that completes us all. We find ourself at the doorway of the new age of love, for love is the most powerful substance in the world. This great power dwells within us and has never departed from us, although it has waited to find its perfect time with us.

Love is the power that can banish hospitals, old age, loneliness, unhappiness, and want. It is the power that can heal the human body, set us free from all bondage; but first it must be set free to work through us. When we know there is only one Power, the invisible substance, then we know it is in the highest Self of every person, it is the Power in every situation and the true meaning of every part of our world. Let it open our thoughts, feelings, and actions and flow from within. We cannot find love or know it until we feel it flow through us. Love must be set free to complete itself in the human form and every form on earth.

Love is blind to faults or shortcomings. Love is blind to color, race, or creed. Love is the heart of the universe; it opens the petals of the rose and adorns the tree with its gift of fruit. It quenches the thirst of the dried-up earth as well as the thirst of the soul. It greets us with the blooms of spring and it lights up the darkness of every night. It is love that soothes the tired body with refreshing sleep. Love is the light that causes us to find our way from the finite, the limited, to the all-reaching infinite. Love is the cornerstone of the new world. Pure love is a constant reminder of the one Presence and Intelligence. It is the power of the Creator in action. Love is that which draws and holds every expression of life in its right and orderly place. Love is in tune, in harmony with the infinite. Love is functioning without limits as boundless, immeasurable good, *as life*.

"Love feels no burden, regards no labours, would willingly do more than it is able, pleads not impossibility, because it feels that it can and may do all things."

We are love in action.

CHAPTER IX

Love and Sex Are Universal

Some people are afraid to use the word *love*, lest they be misunderstood. Others talk about love all the time and know nothing about the subject. Love is the most baffling of all powers that move through the human form. We are aware of only a tiny portion of the power in us, a Power so great that it rules the universe.

God is love, and the most powerful expression of God through us is love. We have believed that our greatest gift was knowledge, but we find ourself at an earth-day of knowledge beyond knowledge, and we are still empty, sick, and weary of the pressures of a world of knowledge we have created for ourself. The dark shadow of materialism lies heavy upon us, and again we turn to the mysterious questions of the soul: whence and whither?

We find that many of our youth, those who have come to take our places, reject life and even cast it aside. Many people have been disappointed in the young ones, baffled, shocked, and saddened; yet if we search within our own soul we find that we have a hidden emptiness, a frustration that we have learned to disguise with success, fame, outer esteem, and a frantic climb to acclaim and applause. Our disguise has worn threadbare and our own incompleteness is showing. Perhaps the young see this.

We salute and bless the men of research and knowledge, those who have been on the quest for a better life and for the desirable things that make the physical expression of life seem freer. Humanity on the search has lived from every angle: transportation, communication, education, food, clothing, medicine. Oxygen is the sustaining essence of physical life and love is a greater and more advanced force for inner and outer life. Love is the only answer to the modern world. We have tried everything else. We have not really tried love. The people of this world are turning everything upside down for an answer to life's problems. We will find it; it will be *love*.

Sex is the fundamental basis of the universe. Procreation is a law of God, the secret of ongoing life. Let us see if we can understand the power we call sex. There are two divisions of organisms, distinguished as male and female; "sex" refers to this distinction. Sex is the power to create, the act or process of producing offspring. The living substance everywhere present contains within itself the mystery of reproduction. Sex is the mystery of all life, yet common to all, for it is present in every form of life. The object of the sex function is to unite two principles, male and female, toward formation of one new, complete being. Sex, as we have experienced it, is not always an act of love; it can be devoid of love. It is a vibratory action at every level of expression. The most profound relationship between a man and a woman could be called holy oneness—*holy* meaning whole, mental and spiritual, fulfilled in the physical. There is still a completion of love beyond the physical that is not involved with sex at all. Love in its fullness can be a relationship far beyond sex. To say of sex that it is love in completion would be the same as declaring that a small electric light bulb is all of electricity; yet the electric current is present in the light bulb just as sex is present in love.

Love is mankind's greatest possession. Every soul is irresistibly drawn to the radiant ones whose love nature is highly developed. Love is a magnet for good and happiness. Love is the oxygen of the spiritual world. Love never grows less, never grows cold or indifferent, but our awareness of it grows stronger and then we know that it is universal, all-comprehensive, all-inclusive. Love is the way of happiness and the freedom that belongs to God in the flesh. God is love, and love is God. This is the truth, and only as we accept it will we know love and abide in it forever. All love and life come from the invisible Presence within each of us, for they are one and the same in the highest.

We cannot create love by outward effort and appearances. We deceive ourself if we try to create love, and we may be misjudging fascination, infatuation, and outer need for love. Love is not created by an external act, never made holy by words said before a minister, rabbi, or priest. Love is an invisible power that captures and masters us and unites us with the invisible God-power in another being. Love is always present, but it only moves when it feels itself, God with God!

"How does love come? Unsought, unsent. How does love go? It was not love that went." Love is not an answer to an invitation, but a power that seeks itself with such overwhelming force that, complete or incomplete, it never wavers and always satisfies the soul of the human form.

Many people attempt to crush love or kill it, but they meet with little success and great sorrow. One cannot kill God or that which is eternal. The conventions of society, the worldly view of love, the pride and shame of personality, have caused many misconceptions about love. Nothing but the absolute truth about God and mankind—that we are one eternally—can heal the human heart and bring about relationships that will reflect harmony, purity, and heavenly bliss.

We do not need to hurry to see or be with one we love. We are never absent from that one.

There is a heavenly selflessness about absolute love. There is no intrusion of the personal in love, for it is always complete in its pure presence. Let us love those who are the completion of our own soul and keep love high, selfless, pure, and free. Personal love can be restless, with a hunger to touch or contact in some way. Personal love must be one with universal love or it will engender fear, jealousy, possessiveness, and exclusiveness. Let us send love forth, excluding nothing. Love the One in all others. Do not lean upon the love of another. Be content just to love, and let it be forever. It is the *loving* that is soul completion.

Human beings are aware that love brings them their greatest joy, and they try to force it into manifestation by devices such as willpower and sense attraction. This state of expression is back of earthly unions that become earthly prisons for those involved. Love is the Spirit; "the Spirit breathes where it wills, and ye hear the voice of it but know not whence it cometh nor whither it goeth." The wise wait. Love is its own reward, its own joy. Our soul is fulfilled in loving. Love does not seek to possess, nor does it long to be returned; it is content in expressing itself. The command is to love, *not* to be loved. Our greatest reward comes when we love without thought of return. Such love is divine and it never ceases or changes. True love is personal without bondage.

There is a love to which jealousy is impossible, wherein possession of the body of another is not considered, a love devoid of personality, that has the power to fill the world with beauty and holiness, wholeness; that has the power to become universal because it enables us to look at each person as if that person were our lover. Seeing the beauty of love in our own heart and mind, we idealize and bless all mankind because we love. No wonder Emerson said, "All mankind loves a lover," for a lover loves all mankind.

Sometimes there is love that is never spoken but is content with silence. Such love is of the new world and somehow, while we cannot fully understand, we *know* it. This kind of love declares "peace on earth, good will to man." Selfless, universal love is the only power that can bring forth the empire of love on earth. Love sees the living spirit within, not just the outer form, and from the love for the beloved it clothes all humanity. One who truly loves is a gateway for the new world, the brotherhood of man. The Fatherhood of God in our heart means tender care, beyond touch or food or other outer needs. The Motherhood of God is constancy, gentleness, and eternal recognition of the best in everyone. Love is pure, brave, and protecting. Who can exhaust the list of love's attributes?

There is a universal expression of sex that we must come to understand. It is the love of God in all creation. The living substance, of which everyone and everything is created and which is everywhere present, contains within itself the mystery of reproduction. The power operates at every level of expression, beginning with the electron and proton being drawn together to form an atom. With man, animals, birds, and bees the union of two principles forms a new being according to the master plan. From the tiniest plant to the monarch of the forest, the law of love and sex goes on and on, and reproduces.

Even the things brought forth in the outer world by the creative action of man's mind must conform to the law and the mystery of procreation. The union of two principles—thinking and feeling, mind and heart—conceives the idea, nourishes it, and brings it forth. Nothing can come forth without the perfect balance of the two, which is universal sex. Love is this perfect balance between two parts in all creation, and only through the same law of procreation could the material wealth of the world come forth.

We have created an outer human environment through the same law of procreation. When the thinking, reasoning part of our being is separated from the loving, knowing part, and continues to express, its creations are imperfect and they miscarry, for they cannot satisfy man's soul and heart, or his outer needs. We have the love within to restore our own outer expression of life to its original, perfect pattern. We must comply with the law. Always there must be two powers working in love—thinking and feeling.

Everything in the outer world is brought forth by the Father-Mother idea. We are now in the process of balancing the outer world of things with love. Every part of our world and all dwellers therein must be balanced in love. This is the time, and love is the only power that can balance the great mind of man to complete our expression. Man was created to grow and fulfill his destiny, and he will not fail! "Every heart that lives with truth is equal to endure." We must be joined with each other by the invisible power of love to know the vitality and essence of the universe, the life of God. Reconciliation and unity will be accomplished by those people who find identity with all through personal and impersonal love. A new world will manifest by the law of love.

Love is the drawing, creating power. Man and God are one; this knowledge can cause the individual to rise above all conditions that in any way separate him from fulfilling life. *Finally, it will be through love of God and the law of procreation that all people will mate with God, bringing forth the new God-being of the new age, the new man and woman.* It will be through love that we will find the completion of our soul in God. This is referred to as marriage, the bride and bridegroom in the Bible. The new being that is unfolding within us will be born from the union of two principles: God and man, outer self and inner Self, forming one new, complete being, the Grand Man! The outer self of us must

love the inner Self of us with a complete love,
then we shall understand: "What therefore God
has joined together, let no man put asunder."
We shall know oneness. This is the fulfillment of
love on the highest level. This is the conception
of the Grand Man coming into *full* manifestation
on earth.

Our true lover is God within. All people of
the earth learn to love each other by loving God
first, last, and always, *since all are part of God.*
The cornerstone of peace is love, and love is the
assignment of this generation, the fulfillment of
the "new heaven and the new earth" wherein all
humanity is unified. Only through divine love
will the empire of love be known on earth. The
unborn millions will live in a completely new
world, a new and *living* way.

CHAPTER X

Love Yourself First

Do you know that you are to love yourself first? You can never be a citizen of the empire of love unless you lift yourself in your own estimation to a place of dignity and power. In loving yourself you are not lifting yourself above others in the old world belief of superiority and inferiority. You are only doing what is in divine order. You must *know yourself* before you can truly know another. Only as you love your highest Self can you truly see past the appearances that you have accepted as real and used as a measure for yourself.

To love ourself we must refuse to accept what others think is important. No one can think past his own state of consciousness, so what others think of us is not important. "There is nothing either good or bad, but thinking makes it so." We are not to look at ourself in judgment, for we only see what seems to be, not what truly is. We do not need to prove ourself to others, we need to feel good within our own heart and mind. A happy feeling is the simplest evidence of God's presence.

To love ourself is to set ourself free to be what we were created to be. Love and do not try to take care of others; set them free under a law of good far beyond meager and limited care. We will never know the dynamic of love until we try it and prove it.

Love is not a word or a name; it is a flame in the hearts of men and women, in the mind and body of every person. But before it can move through us in its fullness, we must love ourself. We may need to overcome everyone and everything in our mind and heart. To overcome is to flow over, move past all old customs, class differences, prejudices, opinions, and beliefs that separate us from the fullness of our life. Let us commit ourself to how great we are. "Do you not know that you are God's temple and that God's Spirit dwells in you? . . . Glorify God in your body." Love and bless your physical being. Take care of the temple. Love the human self, for it is the outer expression of universal Power.

Since love is the power that holds everything in its perfect place, you are right now and always have been in your true place of unfoldment. Do you ever stop to think how wonderful and beautiful you are, or have you accepted a belief in nothingness? Do you think of how many things you have done and shared with others in the days you have lived? In what we call common, ordinary life the little things of each day are the fullest expression of the power of love.

The realization of life makes every expression at one with all others, beyond seeming difference. Life is the one thing every human being has in common. Order and harmony are our life and breath. Life is like the sun in that it belongs to everyone in common. This new expression of life is above and beyond the divisions and differences that have separated humanity. It means that we shall have the revelation and the knowing that every human being is one with God. All mankind lives in the sun and draws life and power from it. The sun shines on every nation, every religion, every individual equally. It is the warmth of every life and belongs to us all. The sun has been the object of worship and adoration of people all over the earth. Yet no nation, religion, or individual would claim sole possession of the sun. As the sun belongs equally to all people, so does life belong to all of us. We are all at one, yet truly individual. Each of us is the creature he was created to be according to a special divine pattern. We cannot be cut off from all mankind any more than we can do without the sun. The power that holds us close is love. Nothing is sacrificed or lost in love.

Since the new world is based on the invisible Presence, and this One is life and breath, it is in the human form that the greatest development and revelation takes place. It is already taking place in our attitudes, relationships, and ways of thinking. The light of the spiritual world is love, and all shall know and feel the glorious Presence like the shining rays of the sun. *We come back to our own inner sanctuary through love.* Once we feel love within our own being and hear a silent voice of feeling and knowing, that "still, small voice" of God, we can never be alone or afraid again; we are born anew.

It is a *state beyond the rational* to be fully aware and a part of the new expression of life, and to follow the rule of the invisible. We cannot fully understand this with the human senses, so we must look inside ourself and find love. Love is the only answer in our new world. Love knows, love feels, love accepts. Love is the law of God unfolding as man and his universe. Love is not a power *in* man, love *is* man in action at his highest level. In this new commonwealth of God we shall all be one, regardless of race, color, or creed. This does not mean that we will not be Jewish, Buddhist, Moslem, or Greek Orthodox. It does not matter if we are German, Spanish, French, Dutch, Chinese, Japanese, or if we represent any country on the face of the earth. What matters is that we will all have the Gospel, the revelation that every human being is one with God. The God-"spell" will fill our mind and heart.

Love is not a power that can be understood completely with logic and reason, yet we must approach it with logic and reason because we have been deeply immersed in a consciousness of the *mind of man* and its powers. We have shied away from the knowledge of the heart and feeling nature because we could not analyze, examine, explain, and understand these from the measure of the mind and senses. Mankind does not understand except from reason, so come, let us reason together.

That we are at the end of a stage of development is clear and understandable. We have grown and unfolded as physical beings, and we have known phenomenal mental unfoldment. Now the physical and mental are merging with the invisible inner Spirit. The new development will be of this invisible Presence, an advancement of the individual from an inner standpoint that will make all things new.

We have made exciting advancement outside our human form through great mental development. We have made tremendous material and manifest progress. We have built a world that we run with machinery. These are the fruits of man's mind, and for this advancement he has been glorified. He has split the atom and delved into the unknown. We know man's mind conceives through great inner Power and moves forward to advance and unfold. The greatest secret and revelation of this mental age is the power of man's mind. The mind has no limits, therefore man has no limits. Humanity has missed a fundamental truth in finding this great secret. Not only the things that build his outer world come from the womb of his mind, but all things come forth from the mind—all that we are and feel! The power of thought controls the body and is the builder of the state of our affairs. It also has power to destroy. We have proof through biofeedback equipment that we can alter our vital functions—like the beat of a heart—by a change of thought. We can accept failure, ill health, or any condition or situation by thought. Not only can we accept them, but we can prove them with our reasoning mind. We have outer proof of failure, or ill health, or a world in ruins, and we have reasons to back up this knowledge. This world of chaos is not real but passing.

The truth is that with the same thought-power we can bring about ecstasy, wholeness of mind and body, beauty, fullness and completion of the plan that holds our destiny. So, besides the mind being the womb of the things of the world, it has revealed to us the secret of life—the why and how of our everyday life here and now. This great power to think lies within us. As we think, so shall it be for us on every level of our consciousness. Whatever our mind dwells upon with strength and believing, that we shall be, do, or bring forth. We must look inside ourself. There is a power *greater* than thinking—the power to feel, the power of love, the power to change all things.

We are told clearly that God is Spirit, our very breath and life. God's love is the only answer in the new world today. In the realm of Spirit a world of love is a new expression of life, as different from our mental, intellectual expression as we are different from the child we once were.

If we are to reap the fruits of the new world of love, if we are to come into our full destiny, if we would enjoy the true freedom from all limitations that is ours by divine right, then we must remember to *love ourself first*. We cannot be part of a world of love if we feel insecure, inferior, or afraid. Only in the sureness of our own place among our fellow men can we qualify for the new world. Only united can we know the Fatherhood of God and the brotherhood of man. We are "fearfully and wonderfully made," with a divine image at the center of our being.

Know that you were not created to be like any other person on earth. You are complete in yourself. Love yourself, honor yourself, and respect yourself. Listen to yourself and the inner murmurings of your own heart. All true guidance comes as intuition and inner knowing, as feeling and movement within. Give to yourself, take time for yourself. Don't cheat or lie to yourself. Have a deep reverence for the being that you are, regardless of birth, race, wealth, or *any* seeming background. You are a chosen soul for this particular time, and you have a purpose for being here and now! Do not waste your substance or essence by being affected by others. Let "none of these things move you" from your love of self or your love of others. You are important to yourself, to God, and to all generations yet unborn.

Is this assignment too great? Love is the only answer and power for the man and woman of the new world. To love is to love yourself, for you are God. Carry yourself as one who owns the earth, because you do! This does not lead to superiority when we know it is true of every living soul. There must arise in our heart a new song, the song we came to sing: "Love is the only king, the only ruler, the only creator. I am love."

How will this give us peace? How will this take care of the needs of the body, educate our children, or keep us from want? All fear and doubt belong to the mental realm. Such states of mind are the refuse of an old regime that we cannot take with us on moving day. They will be no part of our new life. Remember, we are leaving the old world, full of mental hazards and anxieties, and moving into a new expression of life. The adult does not question or fear or measure life from childish beliefs, nor is the bird limited by the broken shell from which it came. Every soul has a royal birth, since life is the movement of God, not the choice of man. All experiences met are points of advancement, important to our life and destiny. We all instinctively know that we are here for a noble purpose. Love your own God-being first, and all else will be added and fulfilled!

CHAPTER XI

If You Want to Change
the World, Love!

The greatest need of each of us today is to reach out with heart, mind, and hand wherever possible, with assurance and confidence, to all who touch our life.

When we understand the full meaning of Truth, we are *alive* to living. No one comes into our life or affairs at any level except by divine appointment. No one comes but the Father sends him, or the indwelling God Presence draws him. Everyone who comes into our life is here for an important reason and purpose. Nothing is happening without the movement of Spirit.

More than fifty centuries ago men began unfolding a story which is called history—"His" story, God's story. In this story human beings have changed the surface of the earth. We have traveled over the water and earth and plunged deep below the surface of both. We have soared in the air and broken loose from the limitations of gravity. We have visited another astral body far from our place of abode. Our fellow men, who are part of our own being, have watched us in our travels and have heard our voice from outer space.

The God-Being has mastered the blind forces of energy through human nature and its power to think and believe. Mankind covers the earth! We have now arrived at a crisis of growth and fulfillment. We are ready for a great adventure. We are beginning to realize our interdependence and the need for true coexistence. We have moved into a new stage of maturity and unfoldment. It is exciting, exhilarating, stimulating, as well as frustrating and frightening. We hold our destiny in our mind, heart, and hand. We have unlocked doors to tremendous power in great steps forward.

There is an almost breathless feeling in the world today. We may not be able to explain it in the midst of rushing and uneasiness, yet in quiet moments we feel an unexplainable *something*, very still in the center of our innermost parts. The past is past and a new time is at hand, unknown, and yet we feel and know without seeing clearly. It is a great paradox. Everything is happening. We are finally ready to consolidate our steps forward and move into a completely new expression of life.

Mankind is coming of age in soul development as well as mental advancement. Something tremendous is happening as we "tremble." We are awakening with a new and startling awareness of our human family and the importance of everyone to the contribution we all must make. In the past we have tried to unite mankind in many ways—by conquest, by religious conversion, by economics, and technological development. These methods have never been completely satisfying or successful.

The way to oneness and complete unity is within each one of us. It is the only way! *We need each other*. We were created with this need. No one is expendable. This is the secret of the new age of man. We must all be *one* in a deep, inner way that lets all outer growth be natural and true as it was intended to be.

Are you willing to take your place in the development of the human race? Will you contribute? Will you participate, or be a bystander, or be crushed in the move? Let us accept our part in this new expression of life. Let us have a little revolution of our own and dedicate ourself to a new and intensive program. We are going to practice the Presence of God in every thought, word, and action as we go about the everyday things of life, wherever we are. We will share with each other in a full awareness of the living God in everyone. We are going to practice living—living fully and completely.

We are going to take the great gift of love out of the inner wrappings. We are coming out of our own cocoon to radiant living. We will study the way of love as given by our Elder Brother. We have the ability to be experts in living, working, and growing together in a new relationship of power and oneness. We will not knowingly waste a moment of life, for we will be fully awake and will understand how precious is the art of being a human being.

Do you want to be one in God consciousness? This is the real question. Can you love and express with the people with whom you live, work, or move at this time? This is the order of the day in our new world of divine oneness. The most important reason for us to do this is that we are here and we are alive. We have been drawn together at this particular time for a purpose, and it is in divine order. Pascal said that since we are here, "we must wager." A wager is a "gage," something deposited as a security, a pledge. *Let us pledge something to life.* Scripture tells us, "You are not your own; you were bought with a price." Remember, you are expressing God. It is not optional—you must do something about life; you are in it, you are embarked upon it, you are here.

How much do we miss of living? How much of life do we let pass us by? Do we know that the souls of others are crying out for the living touch of love and real life? Do we know that we personally are crying out for life and love in the silence of our soul? The lack of love and true living is the cause of every frustration, and inner and outer sickness is the result. Those around us may be in high places and wear the masks of success, fame, and self-assurance, and still be starving for love and empty of real life. Every human being is hungry for a genuine, true, honest-to-God aliveness. We may fool ourself, but this is what we all are searching for—the fullness of life in ourself and others. Life is living and loving. God is Spirit, and *Spirit* comes from the Latin word *Spiritus*, which means breath and life.

We can all "make believe." We can give the impression that we are secure within as well as without. But we may be lost in an inner loneliness that can turn to panic if we have not found the secret of love and life. Though we may walk and move through crowds, there still may be a lonely and empty place inside us. We may chat with each other with surface talk and never speak of the void within or our endless search for peace. We may tell others everything that is meaningless and nothing of what is crying within.

Let's get together, talk together, look out at each other and in at ourself, unafraid, with perfect trust. Let's take off our false faces. We are all in this together. Let us find our true place above and beyond frustration and live with unhesitating boldness. The past was the past; now let's pledge our faith, our love, and every moment for this strange and beautiful yet unknown world. Nothing can be lost or accomplished if nothing is staked. Doing nothing is cowardice, and neutrality is failure.

Faith-believing, in spite of evidence, is more important than the deadly, weighted life of

"Should I?" "What will they think?" Spiritual life is not listening to the murmurings of the world but to that inner voice. The inner voice is the great unknown God-pattern, unknown to human consciousness but known in the land of the heart and Spirit. We must move with Spirit although we cannot see our way in the outer. If we do not act until the evidence is in, it will be too late for participation. We must be bold and believing to move into the life that lies ahead.

The word *moderation* is used only once in the Bible, but *bold*, *boldly*, and *boldness* are used again and again. "Make no small plans—they have no power to move men's hearts." Life is a great adventure. Love is the fulfillment of life. Remember that refusing to decide is a decision, and sometimes an irrevocable one for the time being.

We have been taught in our outer world that we do not need anyone. "I am self-sufficient" has been the password of life, connected with what we call success. We may say, "I do not need anyone," but while we are saying it our greatest need may remain unfulfilled. Let's not play games with the law of life any longer. *We need each other*. This is true of all, though we may call a person great or small, a success or a failure. We were created for each other and we shall not be complete until we fulfill this oneness. "It is not good that . . . man should be alone."

We need the touch, the attention, the interest,

the impersonal and personal exchanges of life. We cry out for them, mostly in a silent cry within, which is the saddest of all. Living is liking, enjoying, loving, expressing, laughing, and conveying life power. *To live is to love, and to love is to be eager for the moments as they come.* Living is the lifeline of the human soul, as loving is the lifeline of the physical body. Love should never be limited to a handful of people. We have been taught to love one—not just one person, but the real *one* in every person. We must believe in the one innate goodness in all, or we will cut ourself off from God. We were not created a stolid, separate being, like a marble statue in the park. We all need the completion of the invisible Self and its outer expression.

In the new world this need for each other will grow in governments, commerce, food, in all human needs as well as the deeper needs that keep the soul alive and allow the Spirit to express. It is legitimate and natural that we feel, expect, and need human relationships in every moment of life. It is the call of God for God! We were created to respond to God in all expressions.

Love is knowing that God is moving in all humanity. This was what Jesus knew; He defied customs, class differences, morals, and all so-called evil. He defied men's belief in winebibbers, thieves, lepers, adulterers, as well as their belief in blindness, sickness, and death. He was bold because He knew that He and His Father were one. Those who stand off in splendid detachment do not find the fullness of life. Only as we commit ourself to a position in the great unknown of God do we know God as love and love as freedom.

Love is a natural, real, alive, throbbing oneness with others, not just in their presence, but at all times, far or near, known or unknown. Love is togetherness in the invisible, never separated by distance or time, race, nationality, or creed, never cut asunder by outer situations, conditions, or lack of contact. We love one another, we love our work, our ideas, our hopes, and our dreams. We love life! Love is the reason for living, and it must fill the earth.

CHAPTER XII

Beyond Differences

The unfolding pattern of the world today is toward *oneness*! Oneness is the message of our age's spiritual unfoldment. The time at hand is more important than mankind has dreamed or dared to think. Oneness isn't an outer, planned place or accomplishment. This is why it is so real, so important. It is spiritually directed and will be spiritually accomplished!

Oneness is not a denomination; it is not opposed to any form of worship of God, or nationality, or race. The purpose of oneness is for every human being to know his own inner power, which is God, and to live and have dominion over his own life and take his place in the new world of mankind. Oneness is not uniformity. Oneness is freedom of expression and includes every expression of life. Unity never closes another out. A person who lives in the allness of Spirit does not interfere with the expression of another to try to change his viewpoint. That would be trespassing. Every viewpoint is an individual evolution or unfoldment and is right for the person and the time at hand.

The supreme possession of all mankind is beyond race, nationality, and religion. It is life! Life is Spirit. The word *Spirit* is derived from a Latin word that means breath and life. Oneness is not concerned with creeds, dogma, theology, or proof of anything based on the beliefs of the past. The wise of the world want answers to their inner needs and their outer life. People want an answer for *today*. The answer must be here and now. The need is to know how to meet life conditions, the common, everyday challenges and pressures of finances, personalities, and physical needs. The world doesn't need a new theory, it needs more inner revelation.

Every heritage of the past has been beautiful and wonderful, and has helped man carry his faith through the depths and the heights. In every moment of man's unfoldment we find a golden thread woven in the woof and warp of life. This golden thread is one Supreme Power. We may call it God, Source, Mind, Allah, Brahma, Tao, or the Great Spirit. It does not matter what we call it; it is the connecting link between us all. When we find this golden thread, we find God, without beginning and without end. This Power fills man with faith, love, strength, and the ability to feel and choose and fulfill his life pattern.

There is no break in the chain of Truth. The eternal Truth of our Creator underlies all differences. Man has dwelt upon difference instead of likeness. The time is at hand to look to our sameness instead of our differences (which are incidental). "The mystery hidden for ages and now revealed to man" has been hidden in differences.

There is only one Truth, though there may appear to be many. One person says it one way, another declares it in a different way. We have many ideas about creeds, dogma, ritual, and ways to worship, but there remains only one Principle: the eternal presence of God. This unseen power of God is in every human form, regardless of all outer differences. Our race, nationality, and religion are our individual heritage and should be precious to us all. But our oneness with life is above all differences.

We belong to the most exciting generation that has ever walked the earth, and we are rising above our differences to awareness of our oneness. To rise to awareness of Oneness does not mean that we are right and others are wrong; it means rising until we know that *all are right*! We are at a great spiritual crossroads. At this crossroads we find a clear path, a path from which none of us can deviate, a path of Truth, a meeting place for all. All who seek to live in peace and harmony are moving through this crossroads, pouring down this clear path. All are emptying into one pure stream of life, to become one in a great consciousness and awareness of the one supreme Power moving through the life of humanity. As each group comes to join the throng, another facet of this mighty One is revealed.

As we stand at the crossroads and watch others pour past us with their love, faith, customs, symbols, and interpretations of God, we say, "How fascinating and how beautiful is the revelation of God in all men!" It is like looking at the beautiful flowers in the garden: the unfoldment of God leaves us breathless. We do not say how different others are but we are keenly aware of the various ways in which universal Power expresses as mankind. The differences do not make us doubt the Creator of us all, but they bring to us a stronger conviction that this Power is the One, the only One, and has always been that One. Every expression of worship comes to add its revelation to the already overflowing evidence of the one great good in the heart and mind of every human being.

Observing the beauty of all forms of worship makes us understand that the plan of our Creator was that we all be different in outer ways, and still all possess the one gift of life! Can we see the beauty of others and their way of expression? Are we big enough for our time and our task?

This one Power is the basis of all religions in the world. Every living soul has the right to interpret this One as he pleases, the right to call it by whatever name satisfies him. No matter what man calls this Power, how he interprets it, he is talking about God—your God, my God, his God, our God, the only God. Religious differences are man-made. The Zend-Avesta speaks of "the Unconquerable One, the All-Seeing One, the All-Knowing One." The texts of Taoism call it "the Great Boundlessness, the Great Determiner, the Great Unity." From Thrice-Greatest-Hermes, the Egyptian way, come these words: "His being is conceiving of all things and making them . . . for there is naught in all the world that is not He."

If we say, "He is life, love, Spirit," does it matter what someone else may say He is? Does the approach make any difference? Every great religion strives to give this great supreme Power back to man, and man back to the Power.

It does not matter in what words man claims his oneness with this Power. "I am the Lord and there is no other." "Hear, O Israel; the Lord our God is one Lord." The Koran says: "And the words of the Lord are perfect in Truth and Justice; none can change His words. He is hearing and knowing." Does it matter if the Upanishads of India speak of "the One God who is concealed in all beings, who pervades all, who is the inner soul of all beings, the ruler of all actions, who dwells in all beings, the witness, who is mere thinking without qualities"? Or that the Christian Scientist says, "There is no life, intelligence, or substance apart from God"? No matter what words we find in Holy Scriptures of

India, China, the Torah, the written law, the Talmud, the unwritten law, or the Christian Scriptures, this great truth is the same wherever we look. *It is in our heart.* If we want to find it we go within.

Every man walks with God in a path that leads to his highest good and clearest revelation. Every human form is a part of every other form. Why do we close the doors of our mind to our brother, and then build a world we must share?

All differences of humanity now unite to become the Truth of all men, the Truth of the great supreme One, and the revelation of this Power in all creation. This is our age. This is our assignment. We are here to bear witness to the truth of this great universal Power, God. This is the heritage of oneness—every living soul at *one* with all, beyond and above outer, accepted differences. Where we see strife, bitterness, race prejudice, and judgment of another man's expression and interpretation of God, we are seeing the rejected, worthless leavings of an old regime, the passing of an old state of consciousness built on separation. It is the end of that which can no longer rule. Something tremendous is happening—a new race of men and women and a new world of expression is coming forth. The old race, the old world, is outgrown, obsolete.

We have built invisible walls that separate. They are crumbling, and man is crumbling too. He is trembling and fearful, for he has lost his invisible support. Man must hold fast to his belief and convictions and not waver. We cannot stand or live without our invisible support, whether or not we understand it. The beliefs of mind and heart, true or untrue, are what sustain us.

The new way of life does not rob any person of his old way, nor can it dishonor any of his spiritual ancestors. We have all come by many different paths to our modern world. Religion has been the thread of God, taken through the heart and mind of man and sewn into sustaining Power. It has been food for the soul as well as for the mind. The full revelation of the presence of the One will fill each mind and heart. In the fulfillment of our oneness there will be no question of the path by which we came to the present day. The fullness of life is that we are all here.

It does not matter what the priest, rabbi, or minister of any denomination is teaching his people. If he is sustaining them with spiritual food that satisfies their soul needs, this is enough! The secret is in satisfying the soul. What do we know? Beauty and good are for everyone in his own way.

We want only to be consciously and knowingly one with every human form. We would not alter others, for they were created in His image and are evolving and unfolding the likeness of the Creator. We want true oneness for all those who dwell upon the earth. We cannot take away the unfoldment and growth that we are all making. We may call this growth troubles or problems, but in truth it is our assignment that must be finished. Let us walk with others day by day, and honor and bless every experience.

All the walls of separation fall away "as the One who became many becomes One again." All differences melt away as we sustain and love each other. To love each other is the Golden Rule. We are in this age by divine appointment, to fulfill a purpose that includes all humanity, whether we be Buddhist, Jewish, Catholic, Christian, agnostic, unbeliever, or undecided. We are never at any place by mistake. There is no coincidence with the Supreme Being. There is only the will of the great Creator, who is in all, through all, now and forever, by divine decree.

The writing is not on the wall but in the hearts of all human beings: "Move on to your true purpose in the 'new heaven and the new earth.' " We are all in the change. We cannot fall back into the old pattern. Time marches on.

Oneness is the pattern of the new world; the new spiritual God-being coming forth in every soul is a change of great magnitude. One world, one love, one man, one God! Until we are drawn together in love our preordained destiny will not be fulfilled. Above and beyond and through all differences is precious *life*. Life, like the sun, belongs to every living creature, regardless of any inner or outer difference. There is but *one life*, and it is in us all, and it is the oneness that will finally make us all safe and free. We do not try to change our heritage. We recognize the importance of life above and beyond the past. "Life is a vital force lying back of, in, and through all created form." All we are, can be or do, is sustained by this vital force. Life is not changed or inhibited by any differences. We are life in action. To *know*, we must feel life in our own body and know that it is the one Power! Let us have an unlimited self, giving love and compassion, flowing freely toward all creatures that live.

> "Earth shall be fair, and all
>   Her folk be one.
> Not until that hour shall
>   God's whole will be done."
>   —*Clifford Bax*

CHAPTER XIII

Freedom from the Past

As human beings we are expressing a divine pattern that was created for us in the beginning. God created all; His creation was and is good, and nothing can be added to or taken from that which God has made. We are in reality limitless. Then why are we beset on every side with appearances that cause us to suffer? The word *suffer* comes from a word that means "allow." We allow, we accept, we sanction, and we permit; in other words, we unknowingly *let* all suffering be part of our life pattern.

We have all said, "I do not have anything to do with conditions or situations in my life." We may add that he or she or the government or our employer, employee, people in high places, or the evil people in the world are causing the conditions. We must know the *cause* of the things that disturb us, if we would change our personal world.

We, ourself, are the cause of all that is in our life. We shall be made free if we accept this truth. All power has been given to us to react to, accept, or refuse all things around us. Our problems are never what others are doing but how we react and respond to people and situations. We are all creatures of habit. We have practices or beliefs acquired by repetition, association, and acceptance. We have all been guilty of saying, "This always happens to me," or, "I knew it would turn out this way." These thoughts stem from habit-thinking. We have expectancy and believing of which we are not consciously aware. They become a part of our doing, unconsciously and without premeditation. Therefore we are unaware that our habit-thinking and habit-acting are the causes of conditions we do not like. We cannot change the effects if we do not know the cause.

We should always be open to the new. Life is constantly filled with expectancy. We should not allow it to be old or familiar, usual or common. We *lose* life when we let it become repetitious and humdrum. What is called old age and senility is really a loss of interest in life, love, giving, and receiving. Mental habits cause cages of thought that close us in. Since everything in life depends on our attitude and re-actions, it is easy to respond in the same old way.

Habits form our whole life pattern, from what time we get up in the morning to what we eat, wear, and how we react to the happenings of the day. If we react with unhappiness, it is easy to *be* unhappy. If we have temporary financial set-backs or physical challenges, it is easy to accept them and look for their return in symptoms and signs. We must always release each experience and be ready for the new unfoldment. Spirit within is movement. Our mind must be renewed, revitalized, and constantly alive to new interests and possibilities. We are meant to "die daily" and be moved into newness of life each morning.

Let's have faith in our own newness. The last promise in the Bible is of "a new heaven and a new earth." We are desperate with sameness, because we were created for movement and life. The true pattern of the mind is toward fulfill-ment of a destiny we have not yet compre-hended. Our old habits of thinking rob us of peace of mind and the joy of everyday living. Many habits are based on prejudices. We have prejudged and concluded what may not be true at all. Many habits have been taught to us and drilled into our consciousness. Some are beauti-ful, such as thoughtfulness and kindness. Listen-ing to our intuition is a wonderful habit. Re-leasing others to their own unfoldment while retaining the right to be true to our own Self can become a habit. Every habit must keep up with life's advancement; it must never be stagnant.

Old, destructive habits of fear and hate are hard to break, because we cannot break a habit by thinking about it. We must condition ourself to think about something else. We don't truly break habits, *we abandon them*. We cease to sustain them with our creative thought and action. We think about something else and do something else. There is a state of consciousness to support a new world, and we should be dedicated to creating it. Let's make new thought habits of expectancy, new life, and greater advancement.

Form the habit of knowing that there is a Power that created us and takes care of us constantly; a Power that can never fail, "closer than breathing, nearer than hands and feet." Let our habit-thought be of life, our innate nature, our greatest possession. Life is a renewing, recreating power that is ever moving forward. Old age, sickness, unhappiness, and disappointment are not conditions that overtake us, they are old habits of thought that cause us to wait for, prepare for, expect, and dread the ugly. There are beautiful, traditional truths that merge with the new. Still we are told "there is nothing new under the sun," for all is natural and eternal, always has been and always will be, regardless of our awareness.

Some patterns of old are true and unchangeable, such as our love and oneness with God. Love and joy and oneness with each other are forever true. There is never a beginning without an end and never an end without a beginning. This is reality. The new is always there. The unfoldment of the individual is the purpose of life, and this unfoldment is in divine order. It does "not yet appear what we shall be." The heritage of mankind has been carried forward by every human being that has ever walked the earth. This is our purpose for being, to carry on.

Man has used many ways and means to carry himself through growth and unfoldment. These methods of the past are no longer useful, as the supporting stake for a young tree is no longer needed when the tree grows tall. That which has supported and sustained us can do so no longer. We are burdened unless we let go of what no longer carries us forward. The child cannot carry his blocks and toys with him forever.

We have accepted our traditions almost as law and truth, and we have used them as patterns for new life. As far as our progress is concerned, tradition can be transcended. Tradition is made up of beliefs and opinions handed down orally from parent to child. Tradition is akin to stories that have become legends. The dictionary tells us that tradition is the "body of doctrine handed down orally, accepted as revealed truth in contradistinction to the revelation of the Scriptures." Many traditional beliefs can be the icy hands that hold us back.

There are old beliefs, not necessarily true, that the body is evil and unclean, just flesh which must die. Limitation of all kinds, accepted as gospel truth, may be proved to be completely false. The belief in two equal powers—good and evil—handed down through the ages, may be resolved in understanding our consciousness of knowing and not knowing.

Tradition has carried the belief in war, overcoming evil with evil. Many of the great men of the past were warriors. War is completely against the Scriptural teaching of nonresistance. "Do not resist one who is evil." How do we overcome evil with good? By knowing that all power is God! We shall no longer be held back by untruths or old thought-habits. All that holds us in bondage is falling away, and anything that impedes our way shall be dissolved. Our way shall be made clear, for it is the time of the freedom of the soul. Freedom is our destiny. Today our path lies beyond the threshold of the mind and the measure of the senses. There is so much more! Man's outer conclusions are a small measure of his true being.

The paradox of life is that we learn the secret of giving up and moving forward at the same time. It is a being *and* a letting. There is a rhythm to unfoldment, the ebb and flow, the giving and taking of the breath of life, the night and day, the wait and go, the knowing and not knowing. What holds us back? Through God we are moving, and from the same movement of God we are hesitating. Each human being must stand alone and know for himself. Only the soul within knows what is right for the individual. This is why we have been taught righteousness. Righteousness is wisdom, the right relationship with God within our own being, and the right relationship with all that is outside ourself too.

As we let go of our old beliefs and accept the

Truth, we release creative powers hitherto dormant in us; these charge us with a smooth, tireless energy, and give us a sense of harmony and peace. Our way is upward and onward. The secret of this journey is that there is always a way to do the thing that must be done, and a way to remain untouched by passing beliefs and events. We cannot be true to the God-self within and follow the dictates of the past, or of others. Let us turn to the inner heart, the feeling nature that is always true. It is the seat of all conscious life. "Do not be conformed to this world." If our eye is not completely blinded by passing events, we shall know that what is seen is evidence of the unseen. Each of us is a big soul, created by God and prepared by our own growth for this time in history.

Something tremendous is happening to us as we tremble with the changing pattern of life. Mankind is being taken over by Spirit. We do not understand the movement of Spirit with human thought. It is so tremendous, so beautiful and full of wonder that we cannot comprehend it with the senses either. We must make sure that we do not return to the stories and legends of old and become lost in them again. Let us be ready to accept the new being that we are, here and now! There is no unforgivable evil or wrong in the past; we have simply outgrown our former expression of life. The simple truth is that the one Presence *is* all, the all that underlies every outward manifestation. Nothing exists outside this Presence. When we begin to believe in God we have a balance of power, given to us for our use. We are "transformed by the renewal" of our mind.

There is a new, high vibration in the world. We cannot live our old life in the accelerated movement of Spirit today. Let us not hold on to outgrown or outworn ways and beliefs. We must stand in the center of our own being and know that God is life, our life, every life! We must go forward, have every experience that comes to us, move through it, and leave it. Let's quit getting ready to live, and let life have its way in us. The upheavals of today are the result of the redirection of the human race. Let us move into new life and share an adventure!

"What mortals have called life, with its mixtures of good and evil, pain and pleasure, poverty and riches, is but an incident, a diversion, or even an aberration, which we must cease to see as life proper in order to recognize the real which threads and fills us all."

CHAPTER XIV

The Vision

Let us have a vision! We belong to each other, and every human being has always had a vision. Vision is a quality which is "clothed with power from on high." We must not lose our vision in the appearances of the day. This is a time for expansive vision and understanding. Our vision is the revelation of what *always has been and always will be*, and mankind is blessed again with recognition and knowing.

We should have the anticipation and wonder of a child, for a child dreams and believes. Let us become little children in expectancy, and learn to dream dreams and have visions of beauty and wonder beyond all we have seen or read about. We were created for an unfolding purpose, from infant to adult. And beyond that, yet unknown to us, is a greater purpose for us. We do not know now what it is but we do know that it is holy. A great, unfolding creation is taking place in us, and transformation is the next step in our spiritual growth.

We cannot help what is happening to us. We did not plan it, but we will not miss the opportunity to be consciously involved in the movement of Spirit through mind and body. There is a divine purpose and plan for each one of us. *Our responsibility is to carry the vision.*

If any person thinks he is wise enough to change the world by coercion, war, laws, or any outer power or force, he deceives himself. "Claiming to be wise, they became fools." The reasoning and thoughts of the wise are vain.

Let us believe in a complete world even though it has not yet been fully manifested on earth. "For still the vision awaits its time; it hastens to the end—it will not lie. If it seem slow, wait for it; it will surely come, it will not delay."

When we think of the good that man has had, the things that have blessed him since the beginning of time, the things that have come forth in the outer world, we think we have touched an all-time high of development; but we shall find that we have only been playing hide-and-seek with the shadow of the things that are to come. Do we have any idea how great is our power to dream? Our dream is a creative power and we contain the essence of life. *Nothing is impossible to man with God.* Let's begin to dream. What shall we dream? Perhaps of a world that is full of love, like the love of a mother for a child, a man for a woman, a person for his homeland and birthright. Love is oneness, therefore love requires that we have the well-being of every other person at heart.

Is a vision of a human being of peace, honor, and inner integrity, who loves himself and his fellowman with the same love, too great a dream for us? Is a world of peace and power, an empire of love, too beautiful a concept for us? Have we forgotten our great power to dream? Do we know that every dream and hope and belief of good, even if we cannot see the good anywhere around us, is the urging of good within us to come forth and fill our life? Do we know that we could not dream of a better life if it were not even now ready and waiting for us? Do we know that the desire for good within us is the sure promise and proof that in the invisible realm of Spirit, whence all things come, the desire is fulfilled and must be realized by us with faith-believing? Faith-believing is acceptance through an inner quietness and knowing; it is the power to reach into the invisible and dream.

The deep, inner soul of mankind longs for release from the pressures that fill our world today. Can we remember that these are the birth pains of a new self being born? We must be born again! Can we know that the old being must be released, and that this is what causes the pain? The pain we are feeling is the death of old expression, and the labor pain of new creation. We have moved through such changes before; we have left babyhood and childhood. These changes have nothing to do with destruction or loss, rather they reflect the absorption of one form into another. Let us remember that it has been decreed that this world shall not be destroyed, but *filled with the glory of God*, to shine among the suns of the universe ... "what no eye has seen, nor ear heard, nor the heart of man conceived, what God has prepared for those who love him."

The day of the consummation of the new world is at hand. We are the people. We are here in the physical body by divine appointment. There must be a vision in our heart and mind. Our assignment today is to carry this vision. *The conception in the invisible must come first.* Before there can be the fruit or manifestation in the outer, we must hold our vision. Before there is fulfillment on earth, our part is the vision!

All who truly love life, who truly love others and the world in which they live, must begin today to believe in a seemingly "impossible dream." The word *human* means "having feelings that are kind, true, and benevolent for everyone." Let us clothe every soul on earth with love, realizing that love is blind to faults and sees only the perfect and true. Let us draw our mind back again and again to the beauty and wonder of life in every form. Catch this vision and hold it, even though it may slip away from time to time. Hold fast to the vision of beauty in all life and all mankind. Let us dream that every human form has a special place under the sun, and that all true leaders are busy helping everyone to find this true place. All education and research will follow the vision. Let us envision world leaders in every country who have struggled for power and peace and suddenly become aware that every person has within him the same holy One.

Dream of executives of great corporations sitting in conference rooms with immense plans and designs for the development of the riches of the earth and the sky, for the benefit of all. Dream that the future of every child to be born on the earth shall be one of spiritual progress and development, peace and hope.

There will be no more poor, ill-kept people, no beggars, none uncared for, because each within his own being will have found the secret of life, God within. All we can ever want or need is deep within us, waiting to be drawn upon by our need and our expectancy of fulfillment. Each must have his own!

Politicians will lift their thoughts and plans to the true positions of trust for which they are chosen. They will truly carry out the policies of the people. They will look for and find the highest and the best for all mankind, the fulfillment of the unfolding new world.

Great separations are healed. No longer is nation against nation, religion against religion, or man against man. The war cry has died out! Soldiers throw away their weapons, strip off their uniforms, and rush to throw their arms around each other. Who is the enemy? Who is the friend? There is only oneness. Who won? No one lost! The peace of every person on earth is here now, but it takes vision to bring it into visibility. *We* must be the dreamers.

What about the children of the world? Who will take care of the children? Envision the children walking hand in hand, running and tumbling over and over on the beautiful soil of the earth. They slide down grassy hills, they pick flowers; they laugh and shout with joy and freedom. *They are too pure to know differences of religion, color, caste, class—and there is no one to teach them such differences.* "And they shall not teach every one his fellow . . . for all shall know me."

Physicians and doctors are filled with *great revelation*. They have found the secret of this throbbing life within. It is the movement of the Spirit, the living breath of God, the true power of the universe. They know the secret of the mind and the power of the word. They have found that a deep, inner sense of peace heals the body. They have discovered that on the face of the earth, in every herb and plant, is the recreating power of God for all of God's creation, including man. Physical suffering was never the destiny of man. Something not yet fully understood, "eternal life," is our destiny.

The scientist in the laboratory is overwhelmed by the power that he comprehends which gives man all power. He puts his test tubes aside, he begins to search the invisible realm of human feelings, reactions, emotions, and sensations. He examines the beliefs, depressions, suspicions, and dreads that fill man's days. The scientist, too, finds the secret of life: *there is nothing God cannot accomplish through man.*

What about the "bad news" that fills our ears and eyes as we listen and see? The newscasters and the analysts at their microphones, the editor at his desk, are flabbergasted, completely astonished at the *good* news: the world is changing, and no one can dream what it may be, but every member of the human race is one. All are brothers, sisters, friends. Everyone is rushing to love, to sustain, to seek greater ways to serve others, to serve God.

What about justice? How can man be safe without justice? There will be no need for judges and lawyers. There will be none to defend and none to judge. Those who have done this work will reach into fields hitherto unknown, using the power of mind and heart for greater development, the uncovering of ways for richer and more fulfilling life.

All the religionists—priest, rabbi, swami, monk, minister—teachers of every calling, election, or appointment will grasp hands, reach to sustain and support one another, for all are directed by God. We shall honor each religion, each man's heritage, each man's way to completion. No two paths are identical.

Teachers in universities will draw from every student the hidden pattern, the hidden secret in the innermost part of each one, that every soul may move forward on his path and share with all the particular gift that is his to give. No longer will they wander and waste the precious gift of time searching for their right place. Each teacher will feel the awe and sacredness of each new soul put under his guidance for a time.

Lovers will love; they will be one in Spirit and in Truth. They shall declare their oneness and bring forth children; they shall build a home that will be a haven until each child goes forth to fulfill his or her own life pattern. Then the lovers will love the world and the people in it, and fulfill a pattern far beyond the pattern of life dreamed of in the past. The new world will not know old age, but a new maturity and full expression. All men and women will continue to love. Love is not something we put away at any point in life, for *we are love*. There is an ancient belief that at the end of a certain period the eagle moults, and by some unknown means renews its youth. We will live so that our youth is renewed like the eagle's. There is a new being walking the earth, in every human form. Man will return to the soil, from which come the riches of God, and the farmer and the planter will be honored among men. Man is free at last. All are safe. All is complete.

Let us have more of a vision of a world unity of all nations, clans, and tongues held together by the irresistible force of love, which is the power that draws and holds everything in its perfect place. Let us envision one law and truth, given so long ago to mankind and called the Golden Rule. "Do unto others as you would have others do unto you," and *do it first*. Let these words become our breath and life in all we think, say, and do.

Let us envision a world that will be the beginning of the "thousand years" prophesied so long ago, a time when there will be revealed to the heart of all humanity a reign of peace on earth, goodwill to man. Let us continue with this vision day by day until it grows clearer to our mind and heart, until we accept it without question. Hold fast until this vision actualizes in the outer. Everything that has ever come forth on this earth came after this manner, by the power of man's mind, and always the invisible vision was first. The time of consummation and fulfillment in the hearts of men and women all over the earth is waiting to be called forth.

Humanity has been separated by a sense of differences, beliefs in inferior and superior beings, beliefs in races and nationalities. We have become convinced of a state of duality, of good and evil, rich and poor, and through these beliefs we have accepted many forms of insecurity. All must be drawn back together and held close by the bond of universal love. When, by the slash of a knife, one set of cells in a body of flesh is separated from another, the healing power begins by reuniting these cells and holding them together until the life principle recreates wholeness. All mankind is being drawn by one great power, the power of love. We cannot envision what is coming forth, because it is far beyond anything we could conceive at this time. It is beyond all knowledge of man. Let us look through the dark clouds of life and the things we cannot understand to the inner revelation that we cannot see.

Love is the secret of the universe. Hold to the vision of a commonwealth of God in all mankind, an empire of love, until it becomes the manifest actuality of all good in the world of men. What we call darkness and evil is *not-knowing*, and not-knowing disappears before the eyes of men and women of vision. Hold to the vision, whether you think others are ready to receive it or not. Make no estimate or measure of any man's place in the unfolding plan, not even of your own state of being. It is not given to any of us to know how far we have come in spiritual unfoldment. The living One belongs to the masses of men and is in them all! Let us think boldly, speak boldly, and fear nothing. Put no limitation on yourself or on any member of the human race.

The great truth of life that we must know is *who and what we are*! When we know ourself we shall know God, and when we know God we shall know our Self. The greatest longing in every human heart right now is for what religious people have called salvation. This is a much-misused word, since to most people it is associated with the word *saved*. Every human being wants to feel safe and secure. Security comes from *knowing the truth* of who and what we are. The true meaning of being saved is *to know we have never for one moment been lost*. We must know that the Power of the universe never can be separated from itself. We are separated only by the "width of a thought." We must hold to the vision; we must *focus* on the truth of the one Power.

Our vision is that all humanity can unite and become one in heart and mind, in the realization that we are all one life. The great Power within us is the Creator and the creation, the Giver and the gift, the Dwelling and the dweller. Never relinquish this vision, for this is our purpose for being. Let us know this precious truth, our true relationship as children of God. The most important thing in the world today is to believe and share this truth. It is not always possible to share it outwardly, but we must never miss an opportunity to share our vision whenever it is feasible and natural. Long ago there were wise ones to whom the Truth was revealed. There came a time when those who knew the precious Truth commenced to conceal it from others, deciding some were worthy to hear and know and some were not. It was at this point in time that we lost our vision of the Truth. Man forgot his birthright. It was lost to those who did not accept it, and it was also lost to those who tried to conceal it from others.

Dreams are a state of expectancy, anticipation. They are the movement of Spirit. The power to envision and look forward is a great power. The outer world has been made of man's dreams. Let's begin to dream of a new life, a new world, a way of love and peace. Let's dream. Dream of every other human being as an extension of yourself. Do not be too big for daydreams or too sophisticated for childlikeness. Otherwise you will not use the substance that builds your world for your own advancement. You are always your own producer.

Whatever your vision, hold it like a precious jewel. Give your gift of believing. Believe your dream with childlike faith, that every man, woman, and child may have the fulfillment of the vision. *Love shall rule the world!*

CHAPTER XV

Why Meditate?

All the world today is turning toward inner space in search of the invisible One! Since all direction in the days that lie ahead will come from a Source deep within the human heart and mind, all humanity consciously or unconsciously is turning toward meditation. Let us understand meditation and why we meditate, and why it is necessary to man's completion.

Do you know how to meditate? If you can truly answer that question affirmatively, then you will know *why* you should meditate. To meditate is as important to our growth as putting seed into the earth or food into the body.

It is surprising how many people searching for peace of mind and serenity of soul will declare that they have prayed desperately, hoping for God to hear them, and nothing has happened. "Why? Why?" they ask. They have told God what they need and when they must have it. They have even told God how it can be done, and still they have no response. Why?

When will we stop outlining and trying to

force, and let the law of life work in its perfect way and time? When will we remember the secret of life? The secret was given to us almost two thousand years ago: "My Father is working still, and I am working." The secret is that there is something we must do; "I am working" is the clue.

When will we know that the principle of the universe is the law of life and has ways to unfold, fulfill, and complete the whole creation through us? The longings, the needs, and the desires of the heart, mind, and soul await our acceptance this moment. Just beyond this moment there lies fulfillment greater than our greatest expectations. We accept this when we do our part, the "I am working" of the law; when we achieve the inner and outer command. "Be still and know."

We *work* when we become so quiet that we are aware of our breath and our heartbeat, when we are aware of the movement of life in and through us, and know that the outer being and the inner Being are one. We make our atonement. *Atone* means "at one." We are no longer separated (which is the meaning of all sin) when we are aware of our oneness with God. We are truly whole and do all things from that point of knowing. We grow and unfold toward complete fulfillment. Nothing happens by chance; all is under law. We are part of a divine pattern which must make us whole if we are to realize our destiny.

We were not created to beg and implore God for our divine heritage, any more than we are to beg and implore the soil to grow the seed, or the food to build our body. We are told, "Fear not . . . for it is your Father's good pleasure to give you the kingdom." All restrictions and limitations result from our beliefs in outer appearances. Why not look inward instead of outward? Why not get so quiet that we feel the movement of life within? Soon we will realize we are *hearing* with inner feeling, and then will come *knowing* with our whole being. It is the still, small voice which is the movement of Spirit within. Soon we find that we are resting in our true relationship to God, and we trust this inner Power to harmonize with our outer self to move through every experience. We have no doubt or hesitancy.

When we were very young, we trusted our earthly father and believed he could do anything. Our father was the greatest man in the world, and we *knew* he would help us whenever we needed help. It never entered our mind that he would let us go hungry or cold or sick. He was our father and he knew everything. When we were just learning to walk we received some bumps and bruises in the process. We knew we had to learn to walk by ourself, so we didn't blame our father when we fell. Even though our father couldn't walk for us, he helped us to get up and walk again. We had faith in him, and he never let us down.

Is it so difficult to recapture that childlike faith without which we limit ourself? As a child we believed in miracles. That was before we let outer experiences create doubt in our mind. That was when we knew without a doubt that nothing was impossible. Still, with God all things are possible, and *we are one with God*. Move with His power through meditation, and be what you were created to be.

Let us return to true meditation. Let us not speak words without meaning. We declare that God is within us and takes care of all that concerns us. This is true, and yet it is not true for us unless we experience God, unless this knowing has lifted us above fear, anxiety, striving, and struggling. *Unless we know in any situation or condition that all is working for the fulfillment of the highest good, we will not experience the peace that comes with believing.* All power is in the midst of us *now*!

Men and women have become like magpies, chattering and scolding, talking, talking, until communication is mere vain repetition. It becomes alarming when we are disturbed by situations and conditions and the power of the word plays a part in adding to the confusion. There is Biblical testimony that we must account for "every idle word." The word, being the thought of our mind and conviction of our heart, has great power.

The word is powerful, but the silence is more powerful. The silence is the Presence of God. It is the "Be still, and know" of the Psalmist. The silence, which is called meditation, is not difficult or mysterious; it is seeking the throne room of God to be renewed and revitalized for the tasks of the day. *It is not a process of mind.* Through meditation the whole of life evolves; it is the resting of the individual mind for a refilling of Spirit in the form of peace, power, love, strength, wisdom, and understanding. *We do not go into meditation desiring anything; we go in desireless.* We know the good of God, for to be in the Presence is complete oneness.

We need to release the mind from pressures and preoccupation with problems and troubles. These are detrimental to health and life. To do this we must become silent in mind, soul (feeling nature), and body. We meditate or contemplate the stillness, the quietness, the strength and power of the inborn Spirit which is God. Meditation has the voice of Truth.

Meditation is not for specific desires about wholeness of body and affairs, not affirmation or repetition, or trying to change anything. It is going into the Presence that is all the life, wholeness, peace, and power. It is foolish to talk about what is not in the presence of all that is. The "is not" lies in our not knowing. There is no evil or lack, except not knowing God.

We go into the presence of Spirit with an empty vessel to be filled. We do not go with a lot of conclusions drawn from mistaken ideas and opinions. We do not seek this Presence for directions on what should or should not be done. Such an attitude shows how little we know. God had already done all. He has given us love, wisdom, faith, imagination, peace, joy, and the power to express a pattern that He has planted in our heart. He has given us inner directions, impulses, and feelings that guide us to the complete fulfillment of our purpose for being.

Meditation is devotion to a purpose. We are told in Deuteronomy, "You shall have no other gods before me." "Me" is this inner Being. To be focused on this inner power is to set our soul free from the limitations of the world with its turmoil, anxiety, and pressures of conflicting states of mind. To be completely involved in outer things is to deny the presence and power of God. It is to proclaim an opposing power, *and there is no such thing*. There is no power against us. There is only God within, and all expressions of this One without.

Meditation is the silence, the only door to the within. It is the act of withdrawing from things of the world and returning to the Source, from which all power and direction originate. The young especially are turning to it, often to the Eastern version, but meditation itself is as universal and as old as time. The state of meditation brings awareness of oneness with the Father, the I AM THAT I AM. Stop looking "lo here and lo there," for the kingdom of God is within you. Meditation was practiced by Moses as he sat by the living water in Midian; by Jesus when He was "forty days in the wilderness" before He could say for Himself, "the time is fulfilled, and the kingdom of God is at hand." Meditation is the same practice of the Presence used by Brother Lawrence, a monk of the sixteenth century. It is the silence and unity of man with God.

Meditation is the means by which we perfect a conscious awareness of God, evolving to a fuller awareness of ourself. The living, conscious entity we call "me" is our portion of all power to fulfill. To be consciously and completely one with this inner Presence, the Source, is our destiny, the purpose for which we live.

We are one with God. We have accepted this in theory, now we must actually experience oneness. If you say, "I know God is in me and in all," when you are feeling hurt, unhappy, lonely, rejected, poorly, depleted, anxious, and judgmental of others, you do not yet *consciously* know. If you *knew*, you would realize that all that God is and all that He has are yours. All the suffering in the world is allowed, but it is not the law of life for humanity. The word *suffer* means "to allow." There is a place of awareness and knowing beyond physical might and human thinking. When we reach this awareness, healing, freedom, and whatever is needed are the signs that follow.

Meditation is the means by which we go into consciousness of the One. There is nothing secret or occult, strange or mysterious about meditation. There is no problem in meditation.

Meditation is first a pondering, a musing, a contemplation, a dwelling in thought, reflecting on the breath and life that is within us, until suddenly we become alive with the consciousness of the throbbing Presence that we are. The result is new peace and power, complete emotional detachment from the disturbances of life.

Meditation is natural and normal, like sleep, and results in a state of being that belongs to each of us. It is a returning from wandering and wondering to Being. It is an effortless mental, spiritual, and physical experience of peace. We are meditating every time we think of God as the life and spirit within our body. We are this Spirit in visibility, and we cannot be separated from it except by the width of a thought. In reality, we cannot be separated from God any more than a sunbeam can be separated from the sun.

Meditation is to feel deeply about the God we are pondering. Meditation has no time limits; this state can be achieved in two or three seconds and last for minutes or hours. There is nothing mysterious about meditative posture. Sitting cross-legged on the feet is an Eastern posture. Are you comfortable sitting on your feet? The body must assume a natural posture that does not intrude on our peaceful feelings. However, the posture has no mysterious power of itself; the key is to be comfortable.

If we begin our meditation with words ("I am one with God" is a favorite of many), we should try not merely to repeat the words, but to arrive at the real meaning of them. The import, the effects and results of such a relationship, should become alive in our feeling nature. Keep to a central thought until every part of your being throbs with life and oneness. Don't let it become a bore or an effort. If it does, get up and go about your outer duties. No strain or struggle should be present. *You cannot enter the kingdom of God by force.* You can only enter into the Presence with a silent, expectant mind. Easy does it! Don't lose patience. Relax.

During meditation, thoughts sometimes wander in and out of mind. Meditation is to withdraw from simple thoughts and unite them with feeling. Psychiatrists tell us that children should be taught to meditate in kindergarten. Control of mind is man's greatest need, for unity of mind and feeling is the creative power in man. Sometimes when we meditate, thoughts of friends drop into our mind; if we bless them, our meditation will proceed.

We can meditate sitting or lying down, driving a car, or in the midst of a conference, because soon we will be aware that we are always and constantly sleeping, eating, and living in God-consciousness. We do not measure or judge ourself, nor do we make a plea for ourself or another in meditation. Meditation is to enter consciously into the very presence of God and remain as long as we experience complete oneness.

Prayer is to praise God and to release our needs into His care and keeping. But meditation is to *still* the human mind of all thinking, probing, arranging, or rearranging, and to *know* that we are one with the I AM of God. *Am* is the present tense, so I AM is here and now; all power is set into motion for us just as we are today.

When we forget all the techniques of meditation and live in awareness of our true Self, when we express and serve for the sheer desire of love, then we reach oneness. Meditation is retiring into the quiet of the soul and relaxing into a restful peace in which Spirit within comes forth and speaks to the mind. When we reach inner quietness, the power of the universe flows through our being, constantly renewing and recreating. God is the *real* of us. Meditation is not long hours of being drawn within, rather it is the basis for a way of life, a continued balance of the inner with the outer.

We become consciously aware in meditation of working with an inner part of our own whole being. We must meditate that we may become complete in ourself. A life of meditation is not withdrawal but dedication to the Presence. Meditation is renewal in order to move through everywhere-present states of conflict. These are the experiences in which we exercise and grow in wisdom and stature with God and men. All meditation results in the successful meeting of life, not avoiding it. *Know thyself!*

CHAPTER XVI

Epilogue

We talk about a new age, a new world, a new land, and an empire of love, but what we are truly talking about is a new human being. Since the world and all that is in it is the outpicturing of the minds and hearts of men and women, to have a new life the human being must have a new vision and become a new creature.

The world can be no greater than the vision of those who bring it forth.

> "We are blind until we see
> That in the universal plan
> Nothing is worth the making
> If it does not make the man.
> Why build these cities glorious
> If man unbuilded goes?
> In vain we build the world
> Unless the builder also grows."
> —*Edwin Markham*

This new human being has been unfolding for ages. We are moving through a human-divine transition prophesied long ago. All history has recorded our unfoldment and progress. We have come again to a high point of evolution, a change. The only tragedy in life is in holding to what is past and not reaching for the new, the "impossible dream" that lies ahead. To move and meet each day, whatever lies at hand, is our greatest assignment. Today we are a part of a movement of the universe that affects every human form. We belong to the cosmos, the order and harmony of the universe. Every creation has a stirring of greater power, an emergence to a higher form of life. It is not just a physical change, it is the unfolding of Spirit.

Today we are closer to the fulfillment of our destiny than we have ever been before. All answers are within us even while we search in the outer. There is a divine plan unfolding and we are in the midst of a beautiful movement of life. We cannot lose faith because of the outer world of appearances. The law of life is more than man's loftiest achievement or his hated limitation. We do not touch the higher law with thinking or reasoning, but with faith-believing—believing without a doubt.

As we look at the world we know that man alone cannot change it. At this point world conditions are beyond human ability to remedy. We fully understand that to try to change, to reeducate every human being to a new way of life, would take forever. Nothing is truly changed "by power nor by might," not in the outer, not by legislation or force, but only by the Spirit within. That which will change us is already within us; it came with us in the beginning.

This time at hand is not the decision of the human mind but the divine order of the cosmos. We shall go beyond the wisdom of man to the wisdom and power that is God. We do not fully understand this invisible Self but our time has come to prove it. We all have a personal part in the day at hand. We shall leave to God the things that can't be done, and we will accept the truth that with God all things are possible, regardless of any outer conclusions or beliefs.

We have a history of not believing in "miracles." In former times those who believed beyond the measure of the senses were burned at the stake. Those who had any new ideas were often called heretics. The power indwells man— yesterday, today, and forever—and it will fulfill man's destiny regardless of his unbelief. Copernicus, who declared that the earth moved around the sun, was excommunicated for heresy. Galileo was prosecuted for heresy in 1633, because he believed the earth turned. He was ordered to recant what he believed and the authorities of his time forbade the reading of his books. He was made a prisoner in his home for the rest of his life. Giordano Bruno, Italian philosopher, postulated his theory of the infinity of the universe. He wrote "De immenso," which was based on the belief that there was but one substance, one ultimate reality. He was burned at the stake in 1600.

We have let go of the past and now we put faith in our ability to accomplish magnificent things. Let us realize that we have not scratched the surface of what is. We shall become aware of the spiritual power that moves through every mind, heart, and body. The feeling of not knowing and the dissatisfaction in the world today are the first symptoms of a new generation that will rise to new heights.

Our world and conditions are not material, solid, or unchangeable. This is a world of invisible forces moved by one great universal Power. The most dynamic power is through the unity of mind and feeling. We may not believe that our thinking is important, but we are helping to form the destiny of all mankind.

The new world is not an ideal world lying in the far-off future. The fullness of God is in the *now*. The disturbances of today are the falling away of the past, all that we have outgrown and left behind. We will find that the answer to every question is within us. No one can do anything to us or against us. We can only react to others with love and wisdom. Do we want this for ourself? Do we want it for another? Do we want it for our children? We can choose what we will entertain in thought. To refuse to think of the disturbing things and to have a quiet expectancy of the good will dissolve any unwanted condition or situation, physical, financial, or otherwise. To get an inner quietness is to open the door for the expression of inner power.

Quit analyzing problems; quit trying to figure out where you went wrong. Refuse to involve anyone else in the details of troublesome thoughts. Refuse to support negative situations. You need only meet one moment at a time and then let it go. You cannot hold it without holding back your own good. God will take care of all that concerns you.

Accept the simple, profound Truth: what you accept, think about, and keep uppermost in your mind will come forth in your life! Do not give your mind to how the problems of the day can be solved. If you let go of the battle plan and get off the battlefield, the infinite law of life will have its perfect way in you. Don't try to force others to do anything; that is trespassing. Just know that the Presence works only through a mind and heart that are at ease.

Life is the invisible Presence and Power back of all movement in the universe. The unseen is the real; inner space is the goal. The inner is the dwelling place of the soul and holds the secret of life on earth. Life cannot be defeated! "Do not be conformed to this world," for the outer is a passing experience. That which is within us is greater than all that is in the world.

It is never too late; since the mind is the womb of the world, it will constantly create. The power within us is limitless, without beginning or end. There is nothing a person cannot achieve if he believes in God. Let us put our mind on inner longings, yearnings, and desires of the heart. Never relive what hurts your heart or disturbs your peace. Let everything pass to make room for the new and wonderful that is in the present. Do with joy what lies at hand. The new is ready, but we must let the old go.

Our good is not ours because of merit, family connections, race, religion, or outer success. Our good does not come because we are benevolent or good, nor is it taken from us because we have failed. We cannot lose our heritage; we can only fail to know it is there. Let us be swift to love and make haste to forget. Forgetting is the healing balm of forgiveness. Let us be quiet that we may hear all instruction from within.

Our time is at hand. The revelations of the next few years will lift us from a poor, sick, unhappy, or miserable state into the fullness of Godliness. We shall all learn to look through the appearance to the Spirit within and the wholeness thereof.

Do you know how beautiful and wonderful you are? Do you see God in your body? Do you know your body is the temple of the living God? Do you love others? Do you set them free? Do you judge them? There is no commandment that says we must like others or be like them. We are to love them and want them to have their good, set them free to unfold their pattern. Only God in the innermost part of the soul knows what one should do. Let go of all others and live, love, and see what God will do through you!

No power on earth can hold back the unfolding pattern of the universe. No wisdom or knowledge or understanding or misunderstanding of man can keep the earth from turning or the stars from coming nightly to the sky. Divine order will take care of everything.

Religion is a sacred thing and belongs to the individual. It dwells in the heart and mind. The word *religion* comes from an old Latin word for "taboo," which means "set apart, sacred." Our religion, our understanding of God, makes us sacred and individual. Our God-self is ours and ours alone. Each living soul must be one with the power within his own being, reserved for him alone to know, and to this Self he must be true.

Humanity has never been lost, nor has any individual been lost. We can be separated from good only by not knowing. We are impelled from within to go forward. Do not try to find out how the invisible works; it is not given to us to know.

> "God moves in a mysterious way
> His wonders to perform."

No one can prove for another; we must all know for ourself. "If you can! All things are possible to him who believes." Life is for living. All power is ours now!

The truth that will set every human being free is the knowledge that we are all complete in

God. No one can own or possess another. We are total beings. Let us think of all the people that are or ever have been part of our life. Perhaps we were born to them or gave birth to them. We may be married to one of them, or work for them. They may be our best friend, or the thorn in our side. We are one with them, but there is one thing that is not ours nor could it ever be ours. We do not get *soul rights* to another. Every soul belongs only to the God within. We have the responsibility and we have the ability to respond to this mighty power. We have not chosen to live, we have been chosen. Let us be what we were created to be.

Remember the wonderful words that Frederick Loomis found on the wall of an old Chinese garden: "Enjoy yourself, it's later than you think." I say to you, "Enjoy yourself, it's *greater* than you think!" All is well. Today we are experiencing a great movement of the original creation, bringing forth a new human being whose time has come. We are at a point of no return; we can only go forward. *The new way is to love.* It is a way that has never before been followed completely by man. It has never been fully envisioned.

Now is the time; we are the people. The signpost reads, "Love one another."

> "Each soul that has breath and being
> Is touched with heaven's own fire.
> Each living man is a part of a plan
> To lift the world up higher."

A long, long time ago a caveman stood in the opening of his cave and gazed at his world. With his wildest imagination or the wisdom that was his, he could not dream of the world that man would bring forth out of his mind. Today we (like the caveman gazing at his world) look out at the world we have created from the womb of the mind, and like the caveman, we cannot visualize, with our hopes, dreams, or aspirations, even a glimmer of the world that is yet to be. Right now we are in the creative process of bringing forth a world from the living Spirit that dwells within. As man moves into the great God plan to fulfill his physical, mental, and spiritual unfoldment, he will find that the power that completes is *love*.

UNITY SCHOOL OF CHRISTIANITY
Unity Village, Missouri 64065

Printed U.S.A.   135-F-3131-3M-12-78